Learn to Paint

BOATS & HARBOURS

Alwyn Crawshaw FRSA

COLLINS

ACKNOWLEDGEMENTS

Now that I have finished this, my fourth book in the Collins' *Learn to Paint* series, I feel I must thank all the people who, directly and indirectly, have helped me over the years. Naturally, there is not enough space to record everyone, particularly the students whose honest and open questions have helped me to write these books with a straightforward, uncomplicated approach for the beginner and student.

I would like to thank Collins for publishing these books; Royston Davies and George Rowney and Company Limited for their friendship, help and materials; John Youé and his editors for all their advice, and Michael Petts for his excellent photography and adaptability.

Finally, the biggest thanks go to June, my wife, for without her total dedication to my art I would not have progressed this far, and to my children – Natalie, Donna and Clinton.

Alwyn Crawshaw

First published in 1982
by William Collins Sons & Co., Ltd
London · Glasgow · Sydney
Auckland · Toronto · Johannesburg

Reprinted 1984
New edition 1986, reprinted 1987

Designed and edited by Youé and Spooner Limited
Filmset by Tradespools Limited
Colour origination by Intercrom S.A., Madrid
Photography by Michael Petts

ISBN 0 00 412118 X

Printed and bound in Spain
by Graficas Reunidas S.A., Madrid

Low Water, Topsham, Devon, 37 × 48cm (14½ × 19in). Watercolour, private collection

CONTENTS

PORTRAIT OF AN ARTIST
ALWYN CRAWSHAW FRSA

Alwyn Crawshaw was born in 1934 at Mirfield, Yorkshire; he now lives in Devon. He studied at the Hastings School of Art and works in all four main painting media – watercolour and oil, pastel and acrylic colours – but his particular interests are watercolour and acrylic colour. A successful painter, author and lecturer, he is considered to be one of the leading authorities on acrylic painting. This is his fourth book in Collins' *Learn to Paint* series. His previous books covered the techniques of landscape painting and working with watercolours and acrylic colours. He is a Fellow of the Royal Society of Arts, and is listed in *Who's Who in Art* and also in the fifth edition of the Marquis *Who's Who in the World.*

Crawshaw paints what he terms realistic subjects, and these include many English landscape and harbour scenes which have been favourably reviewed by critics. Although perhaps better known for his landscapes – his works have been compared with those of John Constable, the best known English landscape artist – he has always been fascinated by and enjoyed painting boats and harbours. He has been able to develop this interest even further following his move from Surrey to Devon, where he lives only four miles from the coast. His paintings of boats range from such well-known subjects as the *Henley Royal Regatta* and the *Queen Elizabeth 2* to simple fishing boats and humble dinghies. Probably his most famous painting of ships is *The Silver Jubilee Fleet Review 1977*, which is featured in this book and commemorates an aspect of Queen Elizabeth's Jubilee celebrations.

He has discussed his painting techniques on a steadily increasing number of radio and television programmes, both national and local, including BBC television's *Pebble Mill at One.* He has been a guest on independent radio phone-in programmes, talking directly to members of the public about their painting problems. In addition, he regularly gives demonstrations to many groups and art societies throughout the country.

Alwyn Crawshaw's widespread popularity developed

Sparkling Water, 37 × 51cm ($14\frac{1}{2}$ × 20in). Watercolour, collection of Major and Mrs. W. Hunter

after the print of his painting *Wet and Windy* had been included in the top ten prints chosen annually by members of the Fine Art Trade Guild. His paintings are in many private collections throughout the world and are sold in art galleries in the United Kingdom, France, Germany, North and South America, Australia and Scandinavia.

His work has been exhibited at the Royal Society of British Artists, London, and also in Russia and several Eastern European countries, including Poland, Hungary and Romania. He has held one-man shows in Chester and at Harrods, London's famous department store. These shows drew an enthusiastic audience, and his paintings have been acclaimed by both the public and critics. His works have a feeling of reality about them, an atmosphere that at times gives the viewer a feeling, like a faint memory, of having actually been at the scene.

According to Crawshaw, there are two attributes necessary for success as an artist: dedication and a sense of humour. The need for the first is self-evident; the second, as he puts it, 'helps you out of many a crisis'.

Brittany Sea Mist, 51 × 76cm (20 × 30in). Acrylic colour, private collection

PAINTING BOATS AND HARBOURS

Painting boats and harbours is no more than an extension of painting landscapes. Let me try to explain. Unless you are out at sea you will find that some form of landscape will be in your picture. It could be cliffs, hills with trees, buildings and, in fact, almost anything that would appear in a landscape. There is one difference – that your boat or boats would usually be the centre of interest and, therefore, the landscape would be in the middle-distance and background. Consequently, it would not play a prominent part in your picture. I purposely did not call this book 'marine painting' because that conjures up ships at sea and painting the sea as a subject matter in its own right.

I have written this book, first of all, for the student who loves painting and the person who wants to paint and needs encouragement. Naturally, above all, it is for the people who love boats. Some people will say that to paint boats you need to know all about them. To a certain extent this is true, as the more knowledge we have of our subject the more natural our paintings will be, but you need not be a marine architect to enjoy painting pictures of boats and harbours! The more you paint the more you will learn and, after all, you will be learning from an artist's point of view, not from a captain's viewpoint. Your key to painting boats, as with any other subject, is observation.

Don't let technical jargon put you off. You do not need to know all the various terms and words in a seaman's vocabulary, but if you feel better using the word 'bow' instead of the 'front' of a boat, go ahead. If you are out painting and a fisherman starts talking and uses technical words you don't understand, don't try to bluff it out with him. Explain you don't understand and ask him what he means. He will be only too pleased to explain all sorts of technical and nautical terms to you.

Although I have said you can paint without knowing these words and names, you will be surprised how much more confident you will be if you can use some. You could, for instance, show someone your picture and comment that: 'It could have done with a little darker tone on the mainsail, which would have helped the jib to show up more.' This is all illusion, of course, because it will not make your picture any better. It will make you feel closer to your subject; more sympathetic towards it; less afraid of people looking and talking to you while you are working and, finally and most important of all, give you *more confidence in yourself and your subject*. When you are out painting, in the same way that you observe your subject visually, listen to anyone with authority and learn technical terms, sea stories and 'know-how'. Always be ready with an open mind and open eyes to learn and observe. There is a short list of simple technical terms and names on page 64.

You can work out-of-doors in any medium, and you do not necessarily need a large amount of equipment. Here, I am working in oil colour (opposite), pastel colour (above left) and watercolour (above)

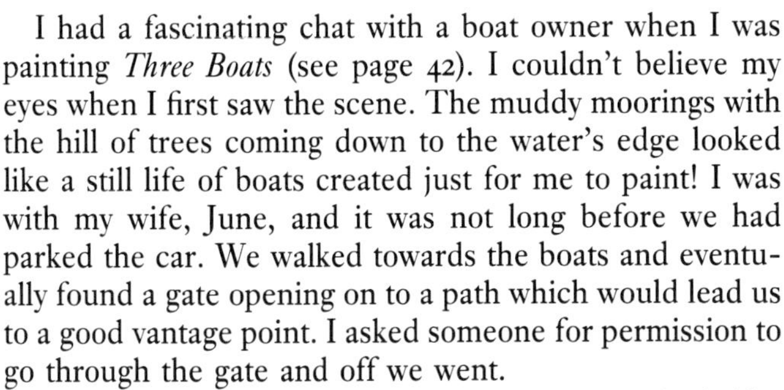

I had a fascinating chat with a boat owner when I was painting *Three Boats* (see page 42). I couldn't believe my eyes when I first saw the scene. The muddy moorings with the hill of trees coming down to the water's edge looked like a still life of boats created just for me to paint! I was with my wife, June, and it was not long before we had parked the car. We walked towards the boats and eventually found a gate opening on to a path which would lead us to a good vantage point. I asked someone for permission to go through the gate and off we went.

After I had been working for about an hour and a half, a man appeared seemingly from nowhere (they always do when you are engrossed in your work, in fact, they can often make you jump a mile, especially when they come up from behind). We said hello to each other and nothing more. I started to talk to him a few minutes later and he was only too pleased to chat to me. People will often only stand and watch, because they are afraid of disturbing the artist, so if *you* feel like talking you must make the first move. Some people are terrified when you actually do talk to them, and look at you in disbelief, because the artist has spoken, and nearly run away!

Let's get back to my painting. I was talking to the owner of the blue boat and he told me it was built during the Second World War and had been a lifeboat on a British cruiser or battleship. It had been unseaworthy when he bought it and he had spent hours mending it and getting it shipshape. He uses the boat for sea angling, and had been fishing in it the day before. The boat on the right had been a tug and used to work around the Dartmouth area. It was being renovated, as was the red boat.

I was most intrigued by the tunnel just above the high-water mark. He said this was an old kiln where lime had once been prepared for the farms.

I picked up one or two nautical terms in our very interesting chat, which lasted for about half an hour. That conversation, with all its information, made my painting come alive. It has given it a lot of meaning beyond an interesting and slightly unusual setting for three boats. All boats, no matter how small or big, have a history and a story behind them. Therefore, there is more to them than planks of wood and pieces of fibreglass or metal.

Most artists are fascinated by boats and have an urge to paint them. Turner and Constable, well-known as landscape artists, also painted boats and their surroundings.

Unfortunately, for a lot of us, the spirit might be willing but actually getting down to a big harbour or far out to sea can be rather impractical and sometimes impossible to achieve. Therefore, I have concentrated most of the work in this book on small boats and harbours, and these can be found all around the coasts and many miles inland. The sketches at the top of page 41 of the large ships were done from a fishing harbour wall, looking out to sea. The original sketch for the *Queen Elizabeth 2* (see pages 56–57) was sketched from a car ferry bringing my family and me back from a holiday in Brittany. If you go on a normal holiday to the coast you will find some form of boat activity, or if you live within a two-hour drive of the coast or a river you can have a day sketching and gathering information to work from at home.

So far we have talked about boats and not their surroundings. In a painting, a boat has character but no atmosphere or mood. This comes from the boat's surroundings and a painting without mood or atmosphere is a dead painting. For example, a boat dancing on sunlit water, with strong shadows and twinkling reflections, conveys a happy, carefree, warm mood. If the same boat were seen in a mist, it would have lost its colour – the reflection, or what could be seen of it, would be very still and the scene would be quiet, still and mysterious.

When you are starting a painting you must decide what type of day it is and how to convey that mood on to the canvas or paper. The hardest part is to keep that mood through all of the painting. To do this, decide what you are going to paint and let your senses be stimulated by your surroundings. It is not only our visual sense that is with us outside, although it is through our eyes that we first see our scene. At the same time, our sense of touch allows us to feel the wind, the warmth of the sun or the sting of the spray from a breaking wave. Our sense of hearing also plays a big part in helping us to enjoy or 'see' the scene: the seagulls screaming; the steady drone of a diesel engine working a water pump or a winch; the wind blowing through rigging lines and, in an active fishing harbour, the shouts of instructions and greetings as boats come into the jetty and start unloading. Above all, it is the sense of smell, along with my visual sense, that gives me the most inspiration for painting boats and harbours. You could be only at the sea or a harbour when you get the smell of salt water, diesel fuel, seaweed, dead fish and crabs drifting past you. Any artist sensitive to nature, who sees and smells a busy harbour scene, could not resist 'having a go' at painting it.

All our senses, then, help us to paint. When you start a painting out-of-doors, let your senses keep reminding you what you are painting. Your visual sense will naturally give you the picture; and touch, hearing and smell will help you to keep the mood or atmosphere of the painting. For example, if you can feel the warmth of the sun you will be constantly reminded that you are painting a warm picture. If you can hear seagulls screaming there is plenty of activity in the harbour and it is not late evening with no one about.

Painting boat scenes indoors from sketches made out-of-doors is a very natural way of painting. Most of the old masters worked outside on smaller studies and used the sketch for information and inspiration for larger indoor paintings. One great advantage of painting indoors from a sketch is that it gives you time to reflect and to consider the progress of your painting, and to change parts of it if you feel this to be necessary.

What is a sketch? The words sketch or sketching are very commonly used in painting: 'I just did a quick sketch'; 'I am going out sketching'; 'I like that sketch', and so on. We have all heard these phrases used by artists, but what is a sketch? The word 'sketch' can mean so much and yet so little. Is it a rough drawing or is it a finished picture? I think we should now define a sketch from an artist's point of view. I believe there are four distinct and very practical types of sketch:

Enjoyment sketch A drawing or painting worked on location, simply to enjoy the experience (**fig. 1**).

Acrylic colour is an ideal medium for outdoor painting, and anyone can enjoy working with it

Fig. 1 Enjoyment sketch

Information sketch A drawing or painting done for the sole purpose of collecting information (detail) which can be used later at home.

Atmosphere sketch A drawing or painting worked for the sole purpose of getting atmosphere and mood into the finished result. It can then be used at home for atmosphere and mood information, or as an inspiration sketch for an indoor painting (**fig. 2**).

Specific sketch A drawing or painting done of a *specific place* for the purpose of gathering as much information (detail and atmosphere) as possible, and which conveys the mood or atmosphere of the occasion. The sketch is used as the basis for a finished studio painting. The 'specific sketch' is actually a combination of the information and atmosphere sketches, but the real difference is that the objective is to go to a *specific place* to record what you see and feel, and then to use all this information for a larger studio painting.

All sketches, whether they are drawings or paintings, can be used as 'finished' works; in fact, some artists' sketches are preferred to their finished paintings. We will cover sketching in more depth later in the book.

The real master for all outside work is Mother Nature. You must never forget this. Try as much as possible to go out and paint. Observe all you can – even when you are sitting as a passenger in a car or train, look at what you see with the object of painting it. When I was at art school I was taught to observe and translate what I saw into a painting (in my mind), and I am still doing this. I could be walking outside and talking with my family about anything other than painting, and I suddenly stop and say to everyone with tremendous excitement: 'Look at that, isn't it fantastic? It would make a perfect watercolour' (or acrylic painting, or whatever medium suited the scene).

Whenever you go out-of-doors carry a small sketch-book with you. If you have a little time on your hands, get out the sketch-book and set about drawing. Try not to miss an opportunity. If you are aware of wanting to sketch, you will find plenty of opportunities coming your way, and if they don't, put a little pressure on yourself and make some: 'If there's a will – there's a sketch!'

I wrote this book to teach you and to help you to paint boats and harbours. I decided not to work in just one medium, but to use watercolour, oil colour, acrylic colour and pastel colour. This will help me to show you the depth and variety of expression in painting this subject. If you want to learn more about these four media, there are four books in this series which are very informative and cover each medium in great detail. They are: *Learn to Paint with Acrylic Colours* and *Learn to Paint with Watercolours* by Alwyn Crawshaw; *Learn to Paint with Oils* by Peter John Garrard, and *Learn to Paint with Pastels* by John Blockley.

In the following lessons and exercises there is no particular reason why a painting is done in one medium or another, although I may have felt that the subject matter was more suited to that medium.

When you are painting try not to get too obsessed with your work or you will miss the joy of being outside and painting. Whatever you do, make your painting enjoyable.

Naturally, there are going to be times when nothing goes right and you will blame everything from your paintbrush to the weather. This happens to all of us, but working directly from nature is spontaneous and something will always be learned, no matter how brief the encounter. *Never* throw away a poor sketch or painting; every line tells a story. If it says: 'Don't do it this way again!' it will serve as a constant reminder!

In 1977, the Queen's Jubilee year, I was determined to paint one of the many great occasions of that year. I finally decided on the Silver Jubilee Fleet Review held at Spithead, off Portsmouth, where the Queen reviewed the fleet on Tuesday, June 28. This 'day out sketching', to put it mildly, gives me the opportunity to talk about my experience of going out to do a specific sketch. It clearly shows the different uses of the word sketch. The Fleet Review sketches were completely planned and premeditated, in contrast to the sketches in **figs. 1** and **2.**

June, my wife, and I arrived on the Monday evening, having checked and re-checked all my painting equipment before we left home. On an occasion like this it is better to take too much than to run the risk of being without. Even if you intend to sketch in pencil, and not to paint, take your paints with you. The circumstances of the event may dictate using them for the best results. In this instance, you could not ask the fleet to do it all again the next day!

Fortunately, we were able to stay with my aunt and uncle in Gosport, only a mile and a half from the sea. Their son worked in a hotel on the front at Lee-on-the-Solent and had arranged a first floor room from which I could sketch the Review. I must admit I was a little bit apprehensive about the number of people involved in my sketching plans, but it couldn't have turned out better.

I had made a point of planning my sketching in advance. I had bought a souvenir brochure, newspapers and magazines and familiarized myself with the total event. One idea I had was to paint the fleet illuminated at night, but did not know whether it would be possible to see it on the Monday, the only evening I would be there.

Fig. 2 Atmosphere sketch

Luck was on my side – everybody agreed to go to see the lights! We set off in the car at about 9.30 p.m., and I took my camera and sketch-book. The road was swarming with people of all ages and sizes heading for the front and, of course, the road was solid with cars of every vintage. Once we had accepted our slow rate of progress we settled down to become part of the crowd and to get into the spirit of the occasion. I got more and more excited about painting the illuminated fleet. Eventually, after more than two hours (we could have walked it in 20 minutes), we turned on to the front, and even found a parking space facing the sea!

The sea looked like a fairyland. The ships were lit up and the lights formed the shapes of the ships. They were twinkling and casting a friendly glow over the sea.

I had planned to sketch in the light from the car's headlights. I picked up my camera and sketch-book and walked in front of the car to take a photograph. Then it happened. As if by some magic spell, as I was looking at the scene with the camera ready, it all disappeared. I was looking into blackness. It had all been so sudden it was hard to comprehend. It must have taken me all of 15 seconds to realize that the fleet had turned out its lights. It was only then that I looked at my watch and found it was midnight – time to switch off the illuminations. I was bitterly disappointed but, as this had not been the main event, the thought of the next day kept me going.

The next morning I sketched from the Gosport end of the fleet, where the *Ark Royal* was anchored. My father, uncle and I set off at 6 a.m., having had less than five hours' sleep. After what we had gone through with the traffic, we decided to walk through Gosport to the nearest sea front. There was activity everywhere. Perhaps it was my own excitement, but I could feel the expectancy of the occasion in the air and all around me. We passed quays where yachts and small boats were being prepared for sea and trimmed with bunting and flags. I felt everyone I passed was out because they had some part to play in the day's activities, even if it were only looking.

There was even more activity when we reached the front. Small tenders were going to and fro between ships and shore, helicopters were buzzing around, and there, in front of me, was the *Ark Royal* with all the fleet disappearing out of my view behind her. The whole scene was breathtaking. I wanted to lift it up and take it home so I could bring it out and paint from it whenever I wanted.

The cool early morning wind blowing off the sea soon brought my artistic temperament down to earth and I began to sketch. I sat on a stool, rested the sketch-book on my knees, and used a 2B pencil. The sketch is shown in **fig. 3**. I knew I wouldn't do my large painting from here but the scene did give me a tremendous wound-up feeling for the rest of the day's work.

Fig. 3 My early morning sketch from the Gosport sea front

After we arrived at the hotel, June and I went on to the beach. I brought my sketch-book and camera and worked on a sketch with a low eye level (**fig. 4**). This was a more intimate work than the one I did from the hotel in the afternoon (**fig. 5**).

The big problem was the weather. The sun came out only a couple of times in the morning, and that looked to be the last we would see of it. This was a problem because the tone of the grey ships made a flat and confusing picture, without sunlight to give them form against the grey background of the Isle of Wight. Under normal circumstances I would have cheated (artist's licence) and put sunshine in the picture, but this was a historical work and I had decided beforehand that if it rained I would paint the rain. The atmosphere of the day was, I felt, as important as the visual element.

After finishing the sketch from the beach I decided I would definitely work from the hotel room. Once I knew exactly what I was going to do the tension in me eased and I started to relax. I organized myself in the room after lunch, making sure everything was at hand. I took some photographs of the fleet but, because I didn't have a telephoto lens, I could not get any close-ups of the individual ships.

I started to sketch with a 2B pencil, working on cartridge paper. From the sketch (**fig. 5**) you can see that I used two pages in my sketch-book. I used binoculars to read the numbers on the ships' sides so I could identify them. This was important as I was near the end of the line, where the frigates were anchored, and I found it difficult to see the subtle differences among the ships, because of the distance at which I was working.

If you look at the morning sketch of the same scene (**fig. 4**) and then at the afternoon one you should be able to see that the ships are facing in exactly the opposite direction. This confused me when I started the afternoon sketch, but I assume it must have been because of the tide turning.

I worked very hard on the drawing, marking the names of the ships as they were recognized – I had plenty of willing helpers with binoculars! I finished just before the Royal yacht, *Britannia*, came past with Her Majesty The Queen on board. I took three photographs and marked with two pencil lines the position in which I was going to paint the yacht. I could not sketch the yacht herself as she passed too quickly.

There were hundreds of small craft moored off the fleet, nearer the beach, and others were sailing, rowing and cruising – most of them with bunting and flags blowing in the wind – in the choppy water. About half an hour after the Royal yacht had passed the cold, overcast weather turned even worse and the Isle of Wight actually disappeared in the heavy, cold mist.

When we got home that evening I felt totally exhausted, but had that fantastic feeling of having achieved something I had set out to do. The satisfying results were tucked away in my sketch-book for me to work from later.

It was a daunting moment when I started work on the large canvas – 51 × 152cm (20 × 60in). The main problem was trying to keep the mood of the day and not to bring in drama with strong lights and darks, as this would not have

Fig. 4 The sketch I made from the beach, before lunch

given the right atmosphere.

The photographs were not very good because of the lens I had used. However, with my sketches, photographs and *Jane's Fighting Ships* for technical reference, I was happy with the result. I often wonder how different the painting would have been had the sun been out – after all, it was the glorious month of June.

This type of sketching out-of-doors is an extreme contrast to a normal afternoon's sketching, but it is a very good lesson in self-discipline and organization to make the effort. You obviously can't wait for another Fleet Review, but you can find plenty of exciting events. There are special boating occasions all over the country, both inland and coastal. Some are famous national events, others are small and local, but all are important and special. They run to a timetable, which means your 'scene' will not wait for

Fig. 5 The sketch of tne actual Fleet Review, done from the hotel in the afternoon

you; you will have to o-ganize yourself around it. If you approach one of these 'specials' in the right way, you will thoroughly enjoy yourself and will remember it. One last point – if you like company you will enjoy the occasion even more if you share it with other people.

Before you start to paint or rush out to find the nearest special event, I would like you to relax and carry on reading this book. I will take you through stage by stage, starting very simply at first and progressing to a more mature form of painting. Enjoy the lessons and exercises. If you find some parts difficult, don't become obsessed with the problem – go on to another stage and come back; seeing the problem with a fresh eye makes it easier to solve.

Remember: *A good painting or drawing is the end result of sympathetic and careful observation.*

The Silver Jubilee Fleet Review 1977, 51 × 152cm (20 × 60in). Acrylic colour, illustrated by kind permission of Mr. C. Brannon, Yorkshire

rowney
cryla
primer
white
PENCILS
Rowney
brushes
Rowney
cryla
colour
Rowney
Willow Charcoal
Rowney
case
Rowney

WHAT EQUIPMENT DO YOU NEED?

The equipment you need for painting boats and harbours is no different from that required for any other subject. You can manage perfectly well with the right basic essentials, or you can fill a room with equipment – it's up to you. I suggest you buy the best quality materials you can afford, to make working easier and to produce better results. A selection of the materials you can use for acrylic, oil, pastel and watercolour painting is illustrated in the photograph opposite, and there is a key below. I have chosen for you basic sets of materials for each of the four media, and you can see these on pages 16–17. These are the basic requirements for each medium and I have used them for all the work in this book.

Colours

Watercolour You can buy watercolours in tubes, or in half or whole pans of colour. I do not advise beginners to use tubes because it is difficult to control the amount of paint on the brush. You can buy pans individually or in boxed selections. The colours I have used are: Payne's Grey, Burnt Umber, Hooker's Green No. 1, French Ultramarine, Crimson Alizarin, Yellow Ochre, Coeruleum Blue, Burnt Sienna, Cadmium Red, Raw Umber, Raw Sienna, Cadmium Yellow Pale.

Acrylic colour There are several types of acrylic colour on the market: the two I use are Standard Formula and Flow Formula. Standard Formula has a consistency similar to oil colour and is ideal for palette knife work. Flow Formula flows – it is much better to use with a brush, and takes a little longer to dry than Standard Formula. Flow Formula is my basic paint, and I have used it for 99 per cent of the acrylic work in this book. You can also buy Texture Paste to help to build up a heavy impasto. The colours I have used are: Coeruleum Blue, Bright Green, Burnt Umber, Raw Umber, Cadmium Yellow, Cadmium Red, Crimson, Ultramarine, Raw Sienna, White.

Oil colour The oil colours I have used are: Cobalt Blue, Cadmium Red, Cadmium Yellow, French Ultramarine, Viridian Green, Crimson Alizarin, Burnt Umber, Yellow Ochre, Titanium White.

Pastel colour There are over 50 different pastel colours, and each one is available in several tints, making nearly 200 pastels in all. Rowney pastels are graded from Tint 0 for the palest to Tint 8 for the darkest. The best way to start is to buy a box of 12 or 36 Artists' Soft Pastels for Landscape. I have used only the pastels in these two boxes for all the exercises. When you get used to the medium you can buy different tints, colours or refill pastels individually.

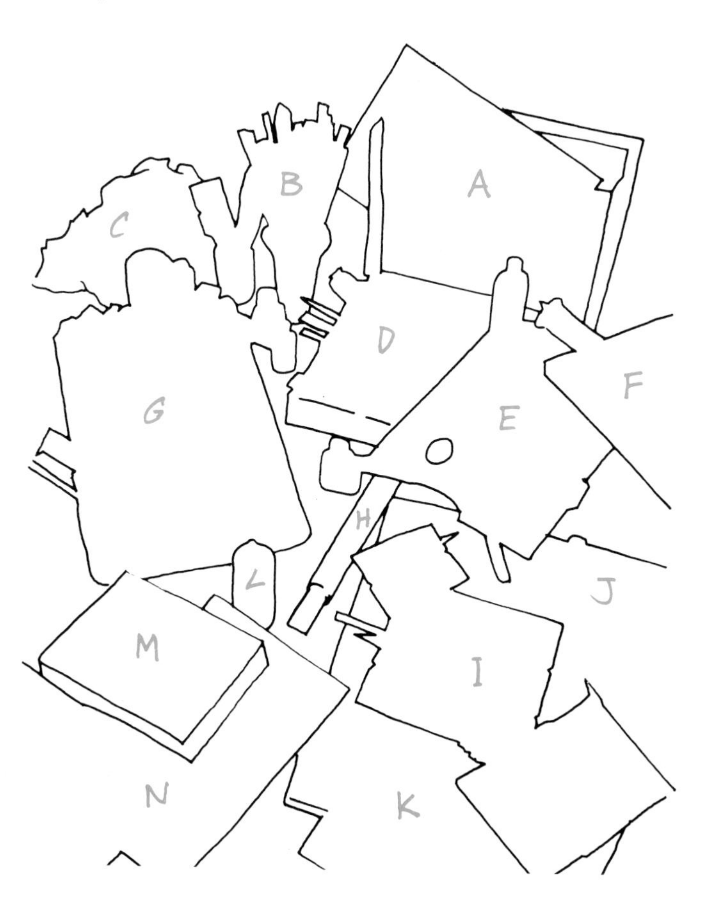

A CANVAS BOARD
B BRUSHES & BRUSH HOLDER
C PAINT RAG
D OIL PAINTING CASE
OIL COLOURS, GEL MEDIUM, TURPENTINE,
LINSEED OIL, BRUSHES
E OIL PAINTING PALETTE, DIPPERS,
PALETTE KNIFE, VARNISH, LIGHT DRYING OIL
F CANVAS, CHARCOAL
G ACRYLIC PRIMER, MEDIUMS, TEXTURE PASTE,
GEL RETARDER, COLOURS, STAYWET PALETTE
H BRUSH CASE
I WATERCOLOUR BOXES, SPONGE,
MAPPING PEN, SABLE BRUSHES
J DRAWING BOARD, PAPER, BLACK WATERPROOF INK,
WATERCOLOUR PAD, PENCILS
K KNEADABLE PUTTY RUBBER, MIXING PALETTE,
BLOTTING PAPER, WHITE DESIGNERS' GOUACHE
L FIXATIVE SPRAY
M BOX OF 36 LANDSCAPE PASTELS
N PASTEL PAPER & SKETCH-PAD,
SOFT DUSTING BRUSH, PASTELS

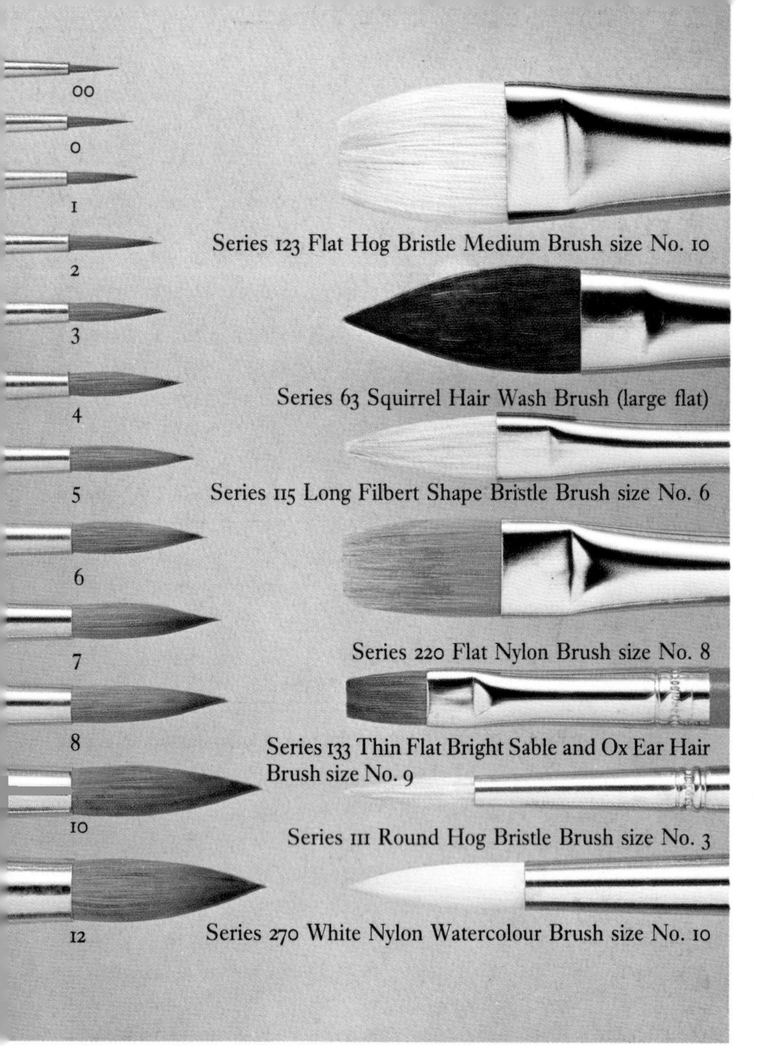

Fig. 6

Brushes

I believe the most important 'tool' that an artist uses is his brush – or painting knife. The brush is the means by which the painted effects are applied. If you want a particular effect, whether bold or delicate, it is your brush that will dictate the result. Therefore, I cannot stress too much the importance of buying the best brushes that you can afford. In the beginners' basic sketching sets listed on these pages I have suggested what you need to start with (the series numbers refer to the Rowney catalogue and will help you to identify the different types of brush). In **fig. 6** there is a selection of brushes which shows the different shapes, types of 'hair' and sizes. They are all reproduced actual size. The brushes on the left are round sable brushes, from size No. 00 to size No. 12. Some brush series have additional sizes, i.e. Nos. 9, 11 and 14.

Always look after your brushes. This doesn't mean that you should keep them in a glass case. You should work them and work them hard. A good brush can take a lot of hard work.

Basic sketching sets

Watercolour (fig. 7) You can start with only two brushes: a size No. 10 round and a size No. 6 round. The quality you get will depend on the price you pay, but they should be sable. You need a paint box to hold 12 whole

BEGINNERS' BASIC SKETCHING SETS

Fig. 7 **Watercolour**

Fig. 8 **Acrylic colour**

pans of colour or 12 half pans (the one illustrated holds whole pans), HB and 2B pencils, a kneadable putty rubber (this type of rubber will not smudge), a drawing board with watercolour paper or a watercolour sketch-pad, blotting paper, a sponge and a water jar. Finally, I suggest you carry a tube of white paint with you. I use Designers' Gouache.

Acrylic colour (fig. 8) I have used six brushes for the exercises in this book. They are Series 220, sizes Nos. 2, 4, 6 and 12 nylon brushes; a size No. 6 sable brush (round) and, for very thin line work, a Series 56, size No. 1 sable and ox brush (not illustrated). I recommend that you use a Staywet palette; it will stop your paint drying on the palette and keep it moist. You can use a gel retarder to keep the paint wet on the canvas longer. For a painting surface you can use paper, board or canvas (board and canvas are illustrated). An HB pencil, kneadable putty rubber, a paint rag and water jar complete this set.

Oil colour (fig. 9) You will need a box to carry around your paints. The one illustrated takes everything, including paints, except the rag, and also works as an easel which you can rest on your knees. This box can be bought empty or complete with materials. Naturally, you can use an old holdall or a small suitcase. The brushes are Series 123 (bristle), sizes Nos. 4, 6, 8 and 10, and a size No. 6 sable (round). You will need a palette knife, purified linseed oil, turpentine, gel medium for speeding up the drying of the paint, canvas board, palette, dippers for holding your linseed oil and turpentine, an HB pencil, a kneadable putty rubber and some rag.

Pastel colour (fig. 10) To start with use either of the two boxes I mentioned earlier. The one illustrated contains 12 colours. You will need some paper or a pastel sketch-pad with a selection of coloured sheets. You will also need some fixative, a bristle brush for rubbing out areas of pastel, a kneadable putty rubber, an HB or 2B pencil and a piece of rag for cleaning your hands.

There are too many different types of paper for me to explain them to you in the limited space here. If you do not understand what the name of a specific paper I mention means, ask someone in an artists' supply shop to help you.

Materials are a very personal choice and your likes and dislikes will emerge through hours of practical experience and experiment. I know it is difficult for a beginner to have the knowledge, or even the courage, to go into an artists' material shop and buy the correct materials. All the materials shown here are of the best quality available and you can buy them in any good artists' material shop, so I hope that by following my suggestions you won't have to worry too much about what to get. If you are still a bit unsure, take this book along to the shop with you and you won't have any problems!

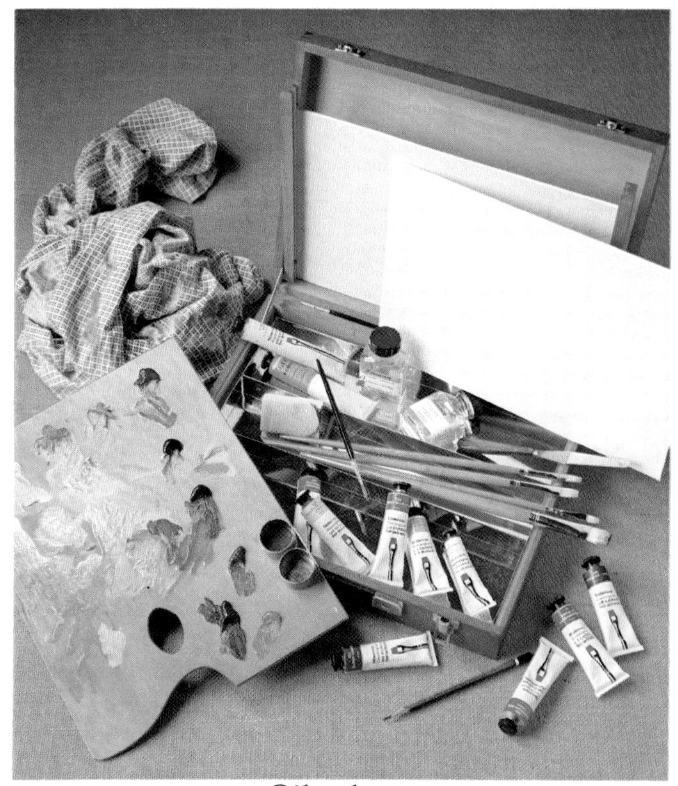

Fig. 9 **Oil colour**

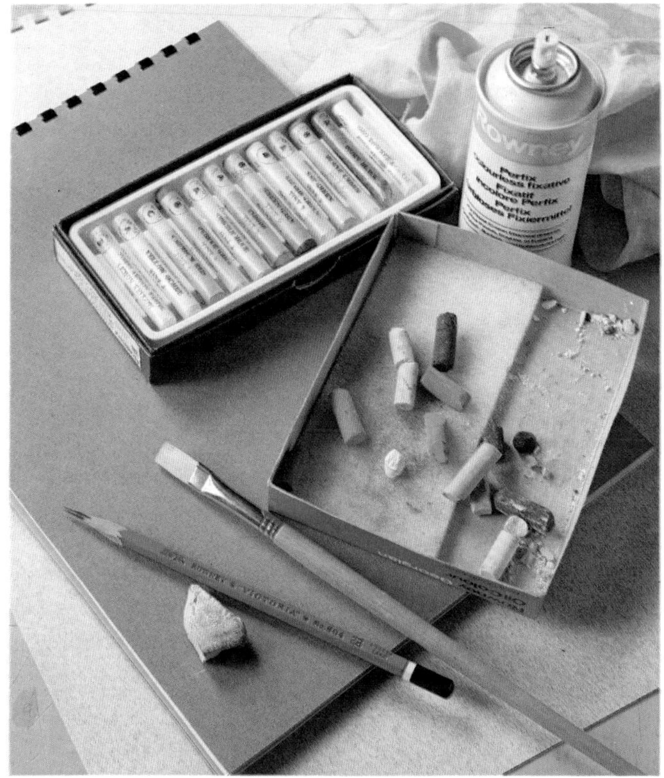

Fig. 10 **Pastel colour**

ELEMENTARY DRAWING AND PERSPECTIVE

A drawing done before painting is the framework on which you add colour to make a painting. It is the guide to what you want to paint. You can use pencil for watercolour and pastel, and charcoal or paint for oil and acrylic painting. I use pencil. It does not matter what you use – we are all individuals and you will find your own method as you gain more confidence through practice.

If you are just starting to paint I suggest you work in the way I have shown until you can work without consciously worrying. If my way is comfortable for you, then carry on using my methods, but if you start to drift naturally into other ways of working, let it happen. You won't have broken any rules.

I am often asked: 'Must I be able to draw to paint pictures?' The broad answer is 'no', but you must have a simple, basic knowledge of perspective and understand that the more accurate detail you want in a picture, the more drawing ability you will need. However, detail can be suggested or you can paint an impression of it, and this does not necessarily call for great 'drawing' skills.

Let us look at the very basic rules of perspective. Most of us are familiar with horizon, eye level and vanishing point, but how do these terms relate to drawing?

The horizon will always be at your eye level when you look out to sea, even if you climb a cliff or lie flat on the sand. Hold a pencil at arm's length, horizontally, in front of your eyes when you are outside. The pencil will always be on the horizon. So the horizon is the eye level (E.L.). If you are in a room there is no horizon, but you still have an eye level. Do the same pencil exercise. Your eye level is where the pencil hits the opposite wall.

If two parallel lines were marked out on the ground and extended to the horizon, they would come together at the vanishing point (V.P.). Railway lines, as you know, appear to get closer together and finally meet in the distance – at the vanishing point.

In **fig. 11A** I have drawn an orange rectangle and a line above it representing the eye level. At the left-hand end of the eye level I made a mark, the vanishing point (V.P.). With a ruler, I drew a line from each of the four corners of the square, all converging at the vanishing point (V.P.). This gave me the two sides, bottom and top of the box. To create the other end of the box, I drew a square parallel with the front of the box and kept it within the V.P. guidelines. The effect is that of a transparent box drawn in perspective. Practise this exercise, and move the E.L. up and down and change the shape of the box. If you turn the book upside down you will see the box with a low eye level and it will appear to be flying!

In **fig. 11B** I have made the simplest of changes to our box. Draw a line from the top left-hand corner of the orange square to the bottom right-hand corner; then do the same from the other two corners. Where the lines cross is the middle of the square. You could have measured this with a ruler because the square is being looked at straight on, but if it were at an angle (drawn in perspective, as in **fig. 11C**) you could not do this. Next draw a line parallel to the sides of the box from top to bottom, crossing the centre point. Draw two lines from the vanishing point to meet the top and bottom of your central perpendicular line. You have now cut the box in half. Draw a line parallel to the top orange line, further back on the box. Where it hits the edges draw lines down to the bottom of the box and make them parallel to the sides. From these points draw four lines, two to meet at the top of the front centre line and two to meet at the bottom. This sounds very complicated, but if you follow the drawing you will find it quite simple and, of course, you will realize what you have drawn – the bows of a boat, in a simplified way. If all boats and ships were made in a simplified way like this, and we always saw them straight and level, our lesson would stop here, but we have to progress a little further.

In **figs. 11C** and **11D**, I have drawn our orange rectangle at an angle (in perspective). This means you have two vanishing points, one on the left and one on the right. Keep to the methods applied in **figs. 11A** and **11B** and all will be well. In **11D** I have narrowed the stern and cut part of the deck away by using the two vanishing points.

In **fig. 11E**, I have drawn a 'worm's eye view', or should I say 'crab's eye view'? In **fig. 11F** I have added a realistic shape to the ship and in **fig. 11G** I have drawn a small cargo vessel to show how to work out the superstructure.

How do we use perspective when we are out painting? Draw your picture 'freehand' (as you see it) and correct it with mechanical perspective if it looks wrong or, as could be the case, you can't get it right. When you are working out your boat perspective, look for the main straight lines or the average straight lines to use as the sides of the 'box'. Try not to be put off by the subtle curves all boats have.

Finally, practise your perspective on any scrap of paper. You will get a lot of fun out of it and will find when you are out that a boat doesn't look as frightening to draw as it did!

Fig. 11

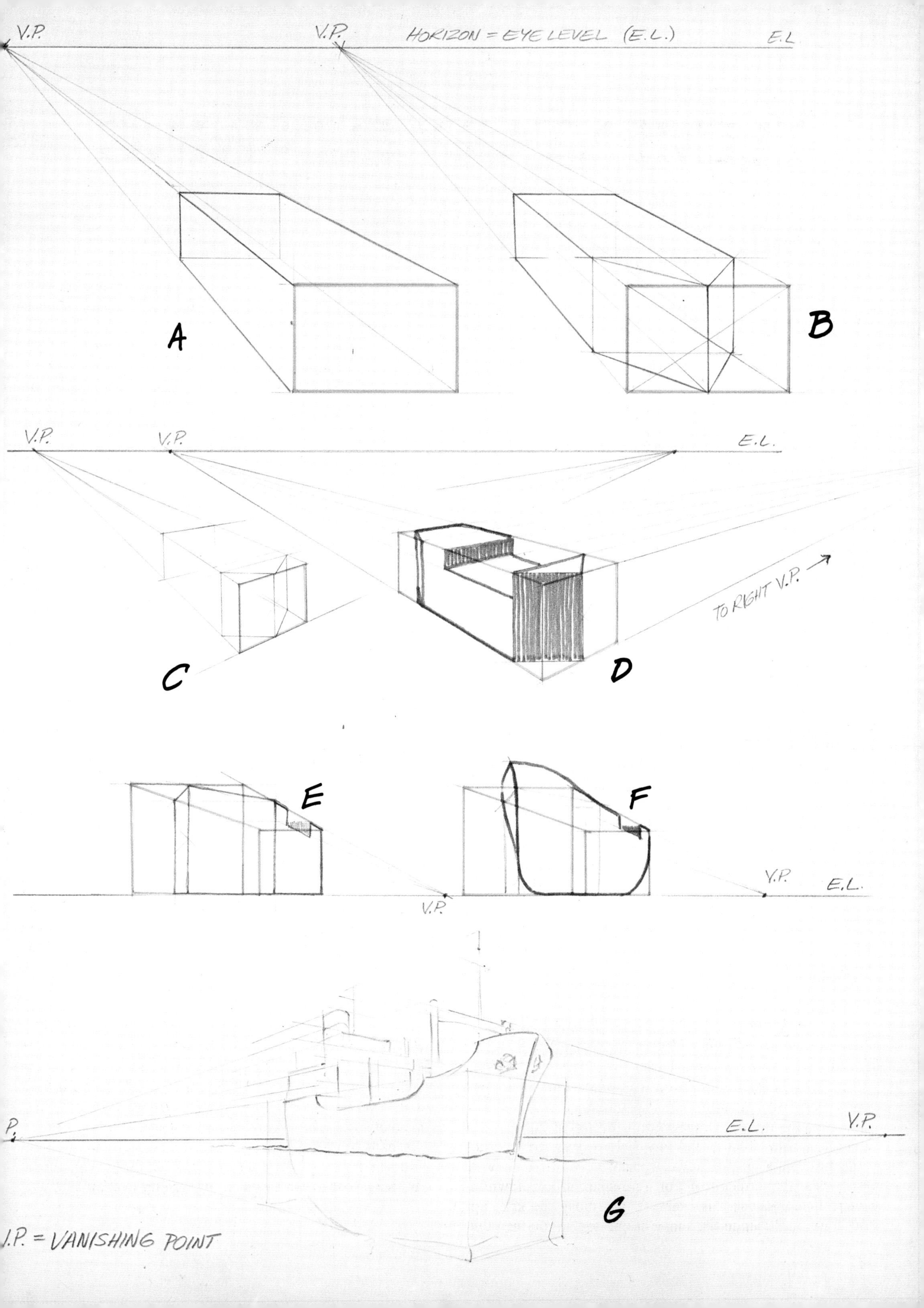
V.P.
V.P.
HORIZON = EYE LEVEL (E.L.)
E.L
A
B
V.P.
V.P.
E.L.
TO RIGHT V.P.
C
D
E
F
V.P.
V.P.
E.L.
P.
E.L.
V.P.
G
.P. = VANISHING POINT

LET'S START PAINTING

PLAYING WITH PAINT

At last you can start painting. If you haven't yet decided what medium to work in I will try to help you. Deciding what to paint with is a very personal choice. Oil colour might be too messy for some people; watercolour too 'wishy-washy'; the quick drying of acrylic colour too difficult to cope with; pastels too dusty, and so on. The previous sentence is really saying that whatever medium you use, you will have to master its own peculiarities, good and bad, to be able to enjoy it. I am sure you will find your own character naturally leaning towards one of them. If you are confused I would suggest you start with watercolour. Under normal circumstances we have all used a water-based paint as children. Therefore, we started by putting a brush in water and mixing into the paint. This, of course, was a very basic method of watercolour painting. Watercolour is also very economical and the necessary equipment is easy to carry around.

Many people who have not painted before find the most difficult part is actually to put paint on paper. This is very natural because whatever shows up from the first brush stroke *only they have created*, and it so often happens that a member of the family (not meaning to hurt in any way) will remark: 'What on earth is that?' or 'Oh dear, well never mind.' Unfortunately, this can upset and put off a sensitive beginner – sometimes for good.

You can't run before you can walk, so let us start by just doodling and playing with paint. Get yourself some paper, from your sketch-pad or anything that happens to be around, and literally 'play' with the paint on it. See what the brush feels like, add more water to watercolour paint, use less water – try anything you like to get familiar with the medium. You will finish up with a funny looking, coloured piece of paper but you will understand the paint and its application a lot more than before you started! You will also have broken the ice and actually started! Do this with whichever medium you decide to use before you try to mix definite colours. **Fig. 12** shows my doodles in watercolour and oil colour. Incidentally, if the family laugh at your first doodles, laugh with them, show them mine and laugh at mine!

Now you are familiar with the paint and brushes, let us take our next big step into painting.

Fig. 12

MIXING COLOURS

You will find this very exciting as you will learn to create your own colours. There are hundreds of colours that exist all around us, but this can be simplified as there are only three basic colours: red, yellow and blue, which are called primary colours. You can see these in **fig. 13**. All other colours and shades of colours are formed by a combination of these colours. There are different reds, yellows and blues which we can use to help us to recreate nature's colours. If you look at **fig. 13** again you will see there are two samples of each primary colour.

In **fig. 14** I have taken the primary colours and mixed them to show you the results. In the first row, Cadmium Yellow is mixed with Cadmium Red to make orange. To make the orange look more yellow, add more yellow than red, and vice versa. Add White to make the orange paler. In the second row, Cadmium Yellow is mixed with Ultramarine and this makes a green. If you then add White, you finish up with a light green.

You may have noticed that my lists of paint colours on page 15 do not include Black. Some artists use Black and others don't. I am one of the don'ts; I believe it is a dead colour – too flat. Therefore, I mix my blacks from the primary colours, as shown in the third line of **fig. 14**. It can be difficult for beginners to get really dark colours at first and, if you get frustrated, I don't mind you trying Black, but do use it very sparingly. Remember that, in general, if you want a colour to be cooler, add blue, and if it is to be warmer, then add red.

As we progress through the exercises I will help you as much as I can, but first you must spend some time practising mixing different colours.

Mix on your palette with a brush and paint daubs on your paper or canvas. Don't worry about shapes – you are concerned with the colours. Experimentation and practice are the only real guidelines I can offer you here. Next time you are watching TV, look around you, pick a colour and try to imagine what colours you would mix to obtain it.

One last important thing: there are only three basic colours, so it is the amount of each colour that plays the biggest part in mixing a colour. You can easily mix a green as in the second line of **fig. 14**, but if it is to be a yellow-green, you have to experiment on your palette; you have to mix and work in more yellow until you have the colour you want. This lesson of mixing colours is the one you will be practising and improving upon all your life – I still am.

Fig. 13

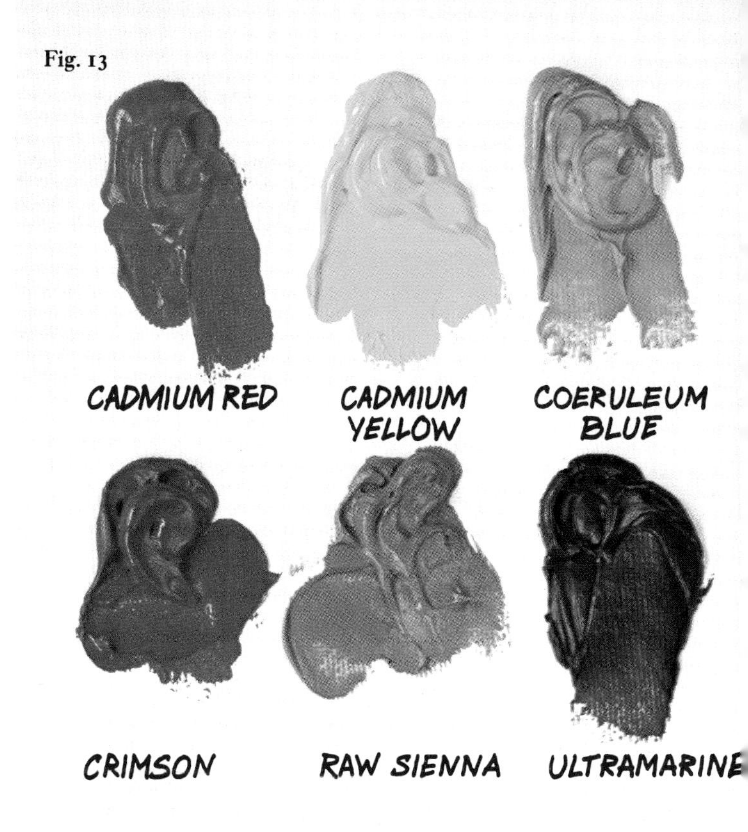

Fig. 14

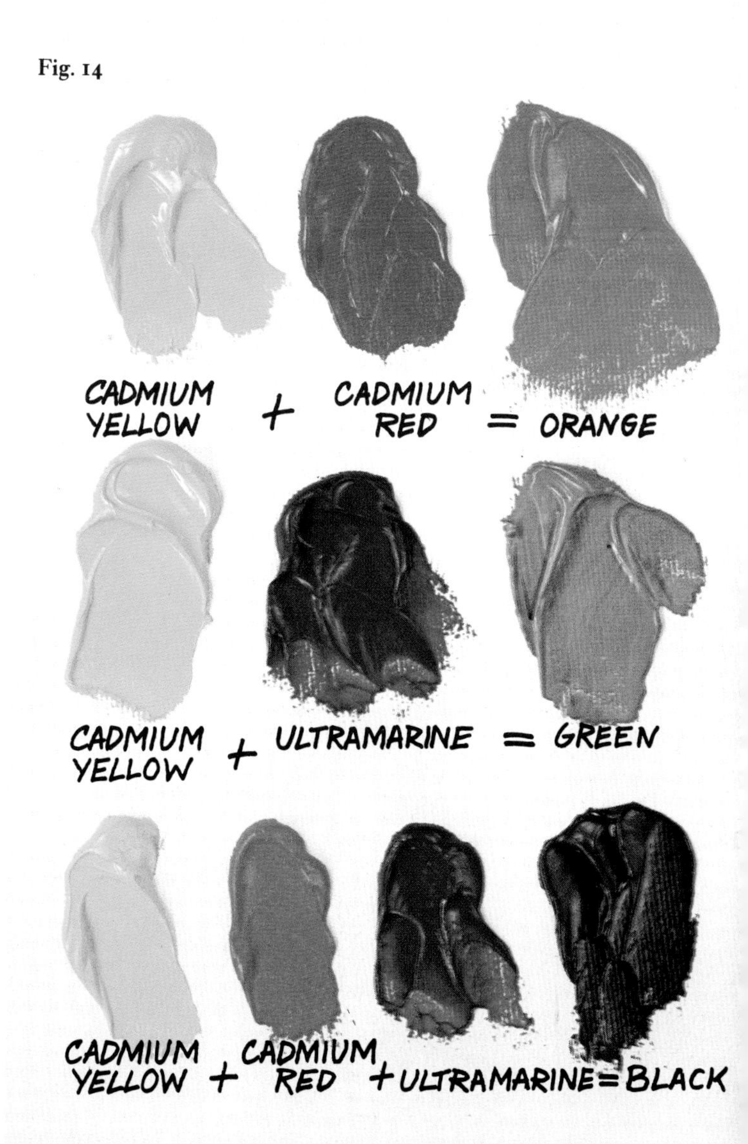

PAINTING THE SKY

If you are confident about mixing colours, you are ready to take the next step and start on some simple exercises. You won't be able to mix every colour you want yet, this will take time and practice, but working on exercises or simple paintings will give you more inspiration than mixing colours and painting funny shapes! These exercises are to be simple – *don't try to put too much detail in them.* If you think I have put in too much detail, finish your exercise when you feel you have gone as far as your ability will take you. Try the same exercise more than once – after all, they are for practice and to give you experience of painting and more confidence for progressing further. Copying my exercises from the book will increase your knowledge of the subject matter, and you will be more familiar with it when painting out-of-doors on location. I said earlier that you must be familiar with your paints, brushes and colour mixing and, naturally, the subject matter is just as important. Remember – confidence comes from being familiar with your work. A good painting will show confidence and knowledge of the subject.

I think the most important part of any outdoor painting is the sky, so I have chosen the sky as the subject for your first exercises. These notes refer to the subject generally and can be adapted for use with any medium. If I have painted an exercise in watercolour, and you are working in oil colour, have a go with your medium. Don't forget that the object of these exercises is to practise and to learn, not to make masterpieces – there is plenty of time for that as you progress through the book.

I have said the sky is the most important part of a painting and I think this is because the sky gives the whole atmosphere to a painting. No matter what the scene is, the sky conveys to us the type of day – sunny, rainy, windy, cold, etc. The whole scene is enveloped in the mood. If you were painting a busy harbour on a sunny day, for instance, there would perhaps be fishermen with no shirts on, sun dancing on the water and holidaymakers in brightly-coloured clothes. You could say the mood and atmosphere came from the busy harbour activities, but every element is affected by the weather, and the sky depicts the weather. If you capture the mood of the day in your sky, it will follow through the rest of the painting. The sky will remind you of the mood as you progress through the picture.

When you feel you are ready to work out-of-doors, forget your paints and use a 2B or 3B pencil, and have a kneadable putty rubber handy. Keep a sketch-book for skies only; it will become a valuable source of information.

Look at a sky for a while and watch the pattern of movement. Observe the changing cloud formations. Half-close your eyes and you will see the sky in a more simplified way. After a while you will have got the 'feel' of the sky and you will be ready to draw it. Start in the middle of your paper – so you have room to work in any direction – and very roughly draw the shapes of the main cloud formations. Then add tone by shading with your pencil.

Even if a sketch takes you only 15 minutes the sky will have changed. If you have been watching the sky and its formation and movement, you should be able to create the design and mood of it on paper, perhaps with a little ad-

Fig. 15

libbing. You should not try to copy every cloud exactly, but aim for an impression of that type of sky. Note the position of the sun, time of day, type of day and date on all your sketches. Don't make these sketches larger than 20 × 28cm (8 × 11in) and you can work as small as 13 × 10cm (5 × 4in).

When you are used to drawing the sky from nature, try it with paint. Naturally, the approach is the same. Use only three or four colours at first, and always add some part of the land or sea to the sketch, to give depth and dimension to the sky. Try pastel colour – it is very good for fast moving skies as it allows you to cover large areas of colour quickly and sensitively.

SIMPLE EXERCISES

The sky in the first exercise (**fig. 15**) is pastel on grey Ingres paper, 11 × 15cm (4½ × 6in). Work Yellow Ochre Tint 2 up from the horizon, and follow it with Burnt Umber Tint 4, applying it over the first colour. In the same way, work Indigo Tint 3 up to the top of the sky. Paint the sea with the same colour. Put in the clouds with short, sharp strokes of Cobalt Blue Tint 2. Finally, add the boat with White (Cream Shade).

The next exercise (**fig. 16**) is a watercolour and I have used only three colours. They were mixed with plenty of water to get the different shades. I used my favourite paper, GREENS RWS 140lb NOT SURFACE watercolour paper, 13 × 20cm (5 × 8in). Wet the paper with clean water. While it is still wet, paint the first stage with a size No. 10 sable brush. Paint the clouds with a size No. 6 sable brush. When the first clouds have dried paint the dark cloud over them with a darker mix (use less water) of the same colours. Put in the hills and boats with a stronger mix of these colours. Practise this type of small watercolour sky, creating different moods and effects, and using various papers, from writing to watercolour papers.

The last exercise, the little 'sun in the mist' painting (**fig. 17**) was done on oil primed canvas 14 × 20cm (5½ × 8in). To make colour mixing simple I used only three colours and White. Work from the sun outwards, using a size No. 6 bristle brush. In the second stage work Cobalt Blue from the sides of the canvas in to the sun, allowing it to mix with the sun's colours. Use circular brush strokes. Finally, paint the boat with a size No. 6 sable. This is another reasonably simple sky. Copy it, and then experiment and practise other sky effects in oil colour. Remember: *the sky sets the mood of every painting you do.*

Fig. 16

Fig. 17

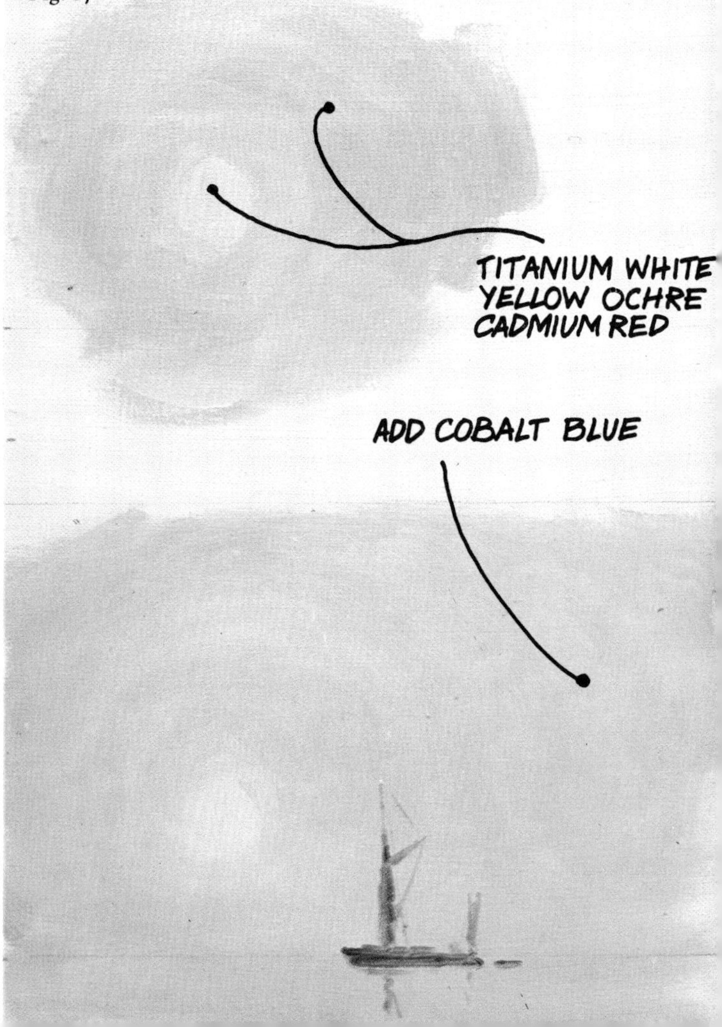

PAINTING WATER

I have always been fascinated with water. I am sure a lot of it comes from the fact that I have loved fishing ever since I was a small boy. At one time I lived at Hastings on the south coast and used to go sea fishing in a small boat. In between bouts of sea sickness (I always got it) and occasional movements with my fishing rod I had plenty of time to observe and sketch the sea. The fascination of water is that, like the sky, it is always changing its mood. Its 'looks' depend on many factors. The prevailing weather conditions help to give water its visual mood, and reflections that are not constant, such as those made by moving boats, change the look of the water all the time.

Water is very exciting to paint and, if taken carefully, you will find it not too difficult to master. As with the sky, observation and then simplification of the shapes and tones are the key. Students are always mystified about the colour of water. The colour depends upon the surroundings reflected in the water, although sometimes the water is self-coloured, for instance in a muddy estuary. Colours in reflections are slightly darker than they are in the reflected object itself. Another point to bear in mind is that reflections become less distinct, and eventually disappear, as the distance from the object increases. Look at the sketch of the large ships at the top of page 41 – there is no reflection. They were about 2 kilometres (1¼ miles) from me, and at that distance you would not see a reflection.

Start painting water in the same way as you did sky. Copy my exercises first, and when you feel confident go out and do some sketching. Use a 3B pencil, the same size sketch-book you used for the sky and find some 'still' water. (Incidentally, you will find a size you naturally prefer to sketch to, and you will achieve the best results by always working to this 'natural' size.) Make sure the still water has some good reflections in it. Sit down, relax and look at the water. If you concentrate, after a while you will see those reflections. If it is the first time you have looked at water in this way you will see that water really is only reflections. Half-close your eyes and the reflections will appear even clearer and more defined, because you will be seeing only the dark and light tones.

When you are confident that you have worked out the shapes of the reflections, sketch them with your 3B pencil. Put in some reflected highlights by taking off some of the pencil with horizontal strokes of your putty rubber. You can also use this method to show ripples.

Next, find some moving water to draw. As you did with the still water, try to work out the reflections. You will find that your eyes move with the water and the reflections keep changing. Again, this must be observed and simplified. The secret is to fix your gaze on one spot on the water – don't let the movement take your eyes with it. As you will see, the reflections stay in one place. They may move a little with water movement but they keep within definite areas. The movement of the water is shown by floating flotsam, water plants and reflected light. Half-close your eyes, fix your gaze on one spot, identifying the reflections and movement, and start your sketch. Try not to fall into the trap of drawing or painting horizontal strokes all over your water. If you put in too many it can look artificial and contrived. Use horizontal lines to give definite effects of water movement or reflected light where necessary.

Never overwork water. When you are painting in watercolour or pastel you can even leave some paper unpainted to represent water. If you are working in oil colour or acrylic colour use your paint thinly, but thicken it for water movement or highlights.

Water with no reflections is easy to see as water when you are there in reality, but when you paint it the effect of

Fig. 18

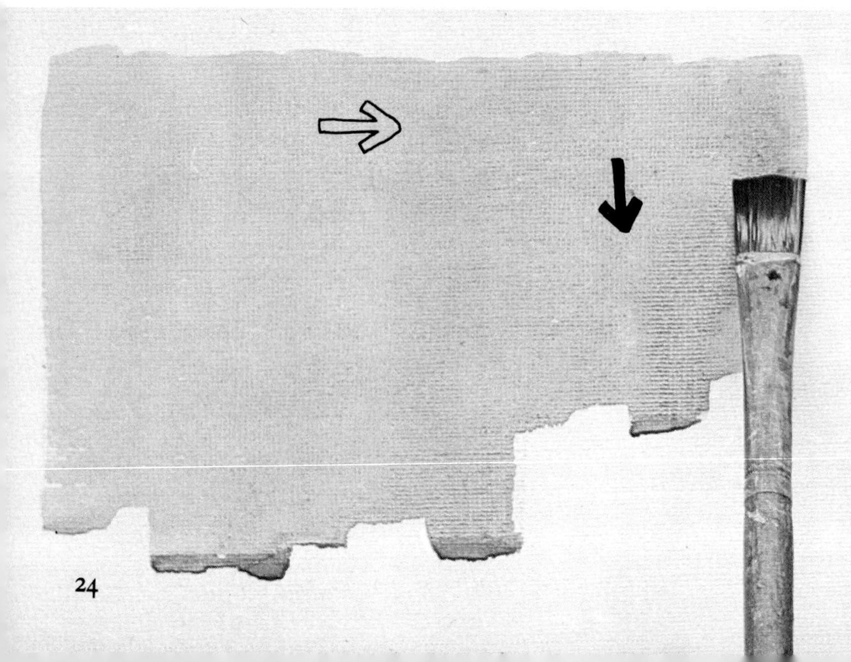

Fig. 19

water can be difficult to achieve. Solve this by adding reflections of your own creation. For example, water left in mud holes as the tide recedes could have some driftwood or an old anchor reflected in it. Use your 'artist's licence' when nature lets you down and leaves you with flat-looking, uninteresting water.

Look at **fig. 18** and you will see two arrows: one is solid black and the other is outlined. *I will be using these arrows in various places in the book to help you to understand the movement of the brush.* The solid black arrow shows the direction of the brush stroke and the outlined arrow shows the direction in which the brush is travelling over the paper. For example, **fig. 18** shows the brush moving to the right after the completion of each vertical stroke. **Figs. 18** and **19** show you how you can very easily give the impression of water with acrylic colours. First paint the water (**fig. 18**) as you would a watercolour wash – very wet. Paint in downward strokes. When it is dry, paint the mud around it (**fig. 19**).

SIMPLE EXERCISES

One of the biggest pitfalls with water is overworking the area, getting lost between water and reflection. As I have said, simplify the shapes. In **fig. 20** I have simplified the painting so that the white watercolour paper is left as water and only the reflections are painted. Do this exercise and then try your own reflections. This exercise was done on watercolour paper, 13 × 15cm (5 × 6in), with a size No. 6 sable brush. Paint the pilings with Payne's Grey and Hooker's Green No. 1. Paint the boat with a mix of Cadmium Yellow Pale and Crimson Alizarin. Next, paint the shadows, using the pilings colours but darker (more paint, less water). Before you paint the reflections, get the tension out of your wrist and fingers by practising on some scrap paper. Paint the reflections with a watery mix of the pilings colours. Don't try to copy mine exactly (that would be impossible) or you would lose the freedom of line you need to represent the reflections. Relaxed brush strokes will help to create the impression of reflections in water.

Fig. 21, painted in oil colour, is a little more complicated as we have to paint some water with no reflections in it. First paint the landing stage with the colours shown. As you work, vary the amount used of each colour to produce the different tones of the wood. Next paint the blue water. Now use the landing stage colours to paint the reflections, as you did in the previous exercise. Then paint among your existing reflections with a mix of all the colours you have used with plenty of Titanium White and Cobalt Blue. Let your paint mix with the reflections in places. Use thicker paint in the lighter areas. This exercise was painted on a canvas board, 14 × 20cm (5½ × 8in) with a size No. 6 bristle brush.

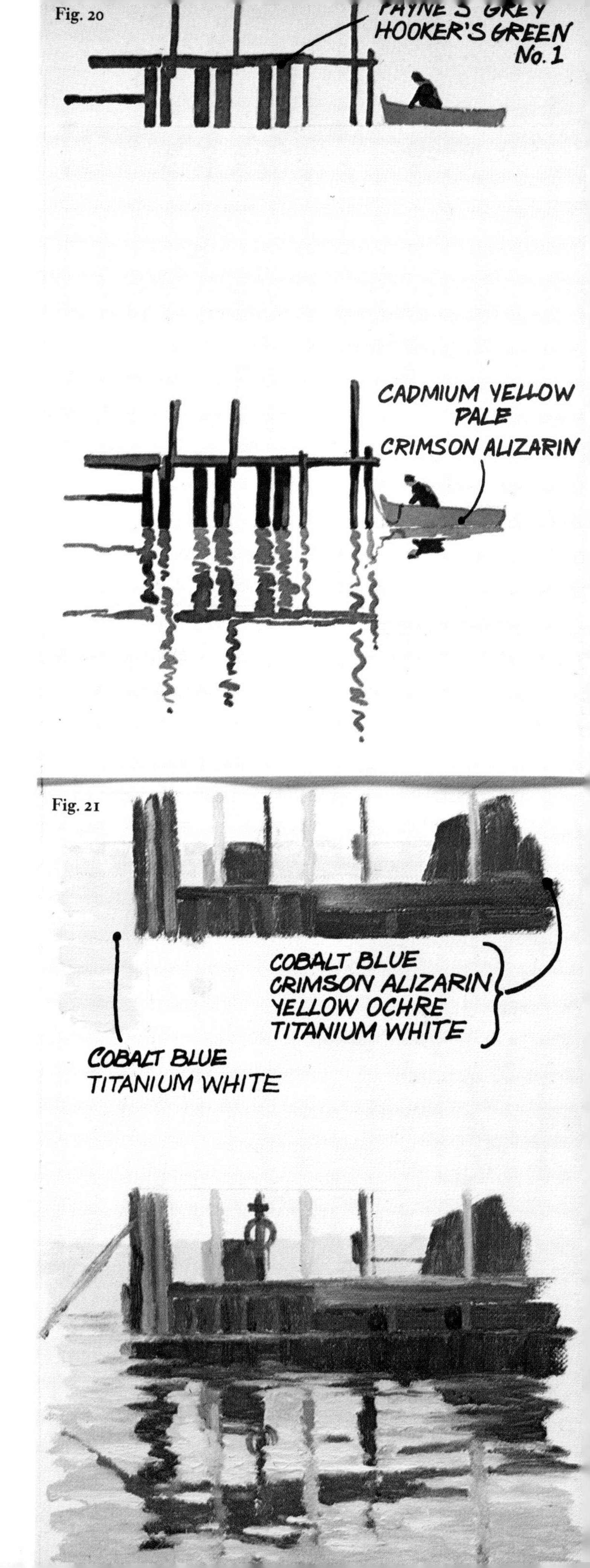

Fig. 20

Fig. 21

PAINTING BOATS

Now we come to the part I am sure you have been waiting for: painting the boats. I bet some of you have had a go already, having seen the exercises on the next few pages. I don't mind if you jump around while you are working from this book, as long as you *do read everything*. In fact, my desire when I worked on these simple exercises was to stimulate you and encourage you to paint boats.

When you start, don't put in too much detail. Try to keep the boats simple – go for their shape and form. What does form mean? Do you remember the old joke of showing someone a piece of white paper and saying: 'That's a white cat in a snow storm.' Of course, you hadn't bothered to paint anything because you would not see anything. However, this is not true because if you did see a white cat in that situation you would make out shapes because of light and shade. There would be shades of white, some light and others dark. If there were no light you would not see any form in an object at all. For instance, think of a sunset just before dark. If you looked at a group of harbour buildings and boats against the sky they would be in silhouette. They would merge into each other and form strange, dark, unreal shapes – because they would have no light on them. Therefore, it is light that gives us form – three-dimensional shape. This is exaggerated when the sun is out, casting strong shadows, because you see light against dark, and they contrast each other.

Let us recap on the last paragraph. We must have light to give us the form of objects. The light casts shadows and produces light against dark and, therefore, we see the shape and form of our objects in three dimensions.

Half-close your eyes and look at your subject. Try the clouds. You do not get much contrast between the greys on 'white' clouds. You will get a better impression of form because the middle tones disappear and the darks appear darker and the lights lighter. Use this method of 'seeing' your subject from now on.

After working on Elementary Drawing and Perspective earlier in the book, your artistic awareness of boats should make these exercises easier for you. Remember to treat them broadly and not to worry about detail. On the contrary, though, if you feel like putting it in then go ahead. The most important aspect of these exercises is to *enjoy them*. If you labour them and worry and fuss over them, you will believe you can't paint boats and they are too difficult.

So relax, treat them simply and, above all, enjoy these exercises. If you get stuck on any exercise, try another one you find easier. Good luck!

SIMPLE EXERCISES

Fig. 22 was painted on Ingres paper, 13 × 15cm (5 × 6in) using three acrylic colours plus White and a size No. 4

Fig. 22

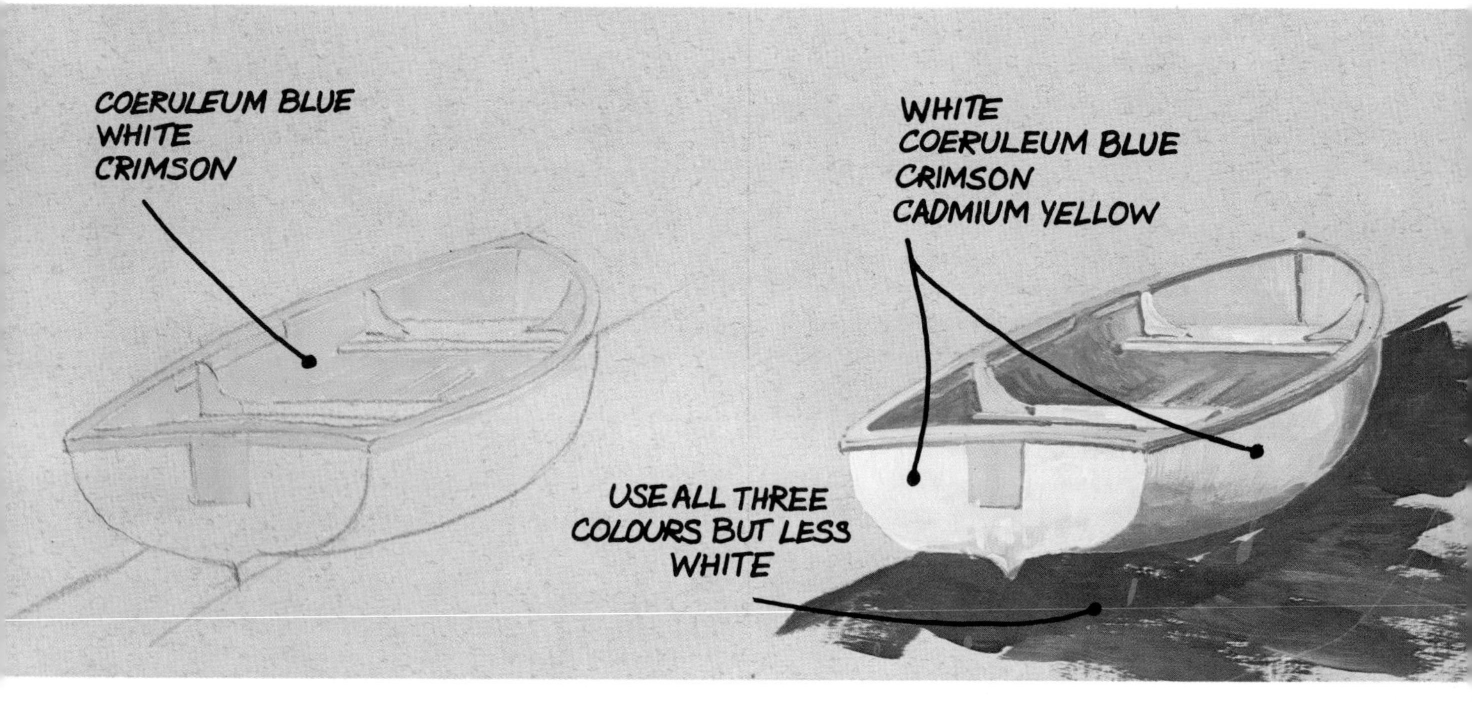

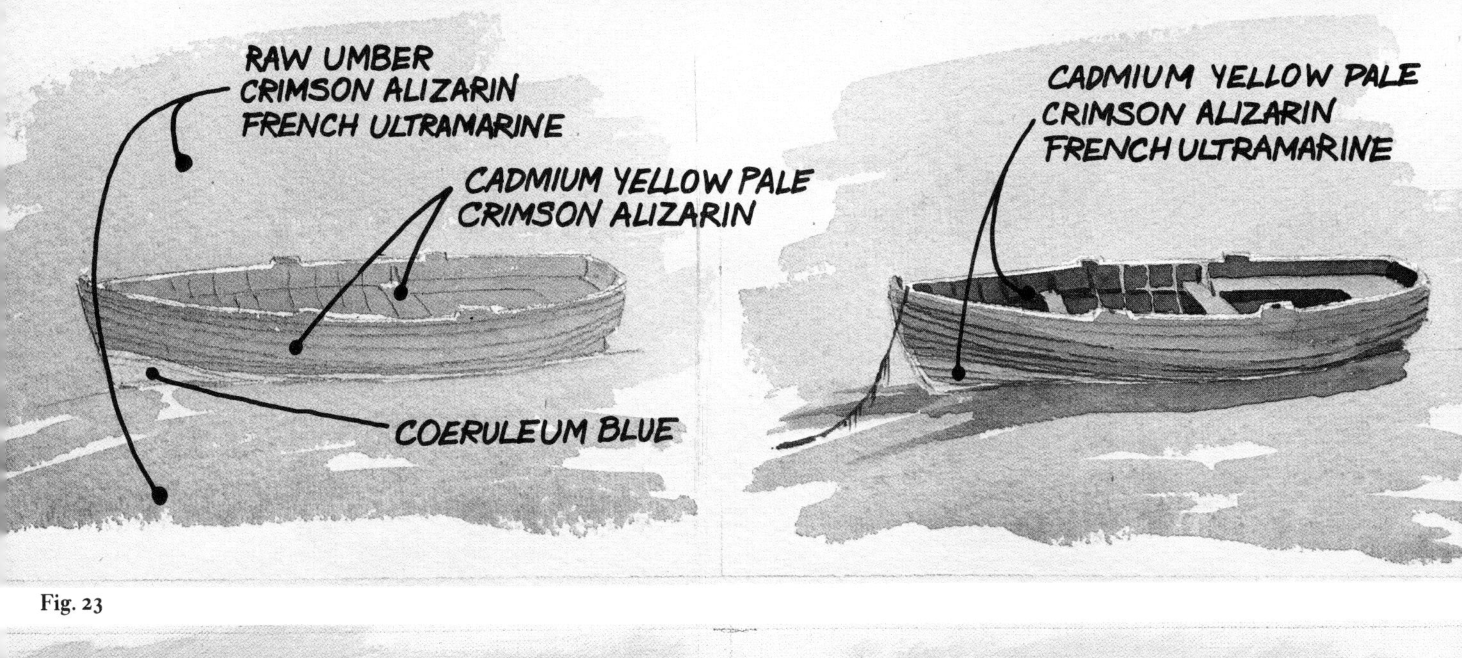

Fig. 23

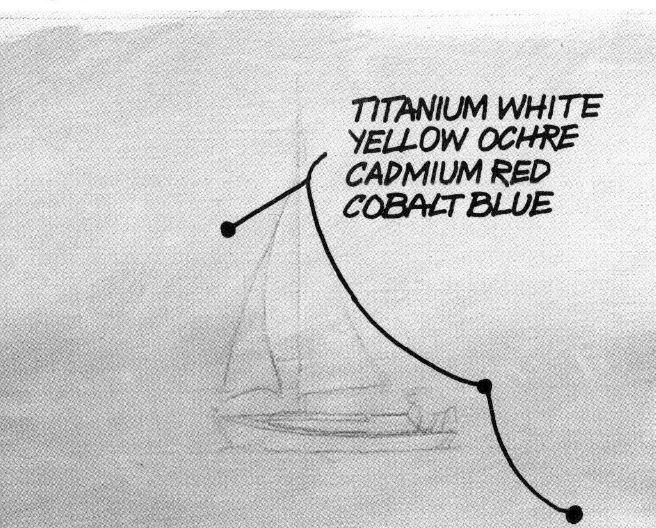

Fig. 24

nylon brush. Follow my painting. If you feel there is too much detail, leave some out.

The next exercise (**fig. 23**) was painted with watercolour. The colours were put in with single washes of colour. Use your size No. 10 sable brush and paint the background first, then the boat and the blue at the bottom. Using the same colours, but darker, and your size No. 6 sable brush, put in the shadows inside the boat and the outside of the hull. Finish with a shadow on the mud. This was done 13 × 15cm (5 × 6in).

The last exercise on this page (**fig. 24**) was done on oil primed canvas, 15 × 22cm (6 × 8½in), using three colours and White. Start at the top of the sky and work down, varying the amounts of each colour as you go. Paint the yacht with thicker paint and add plenty of Titanium White. Paint the yacht while the sky and sea are still wet, and pull some of the sky colour up into the sail area. This helps to create the shadow areas. Use a size No. 6 sable brush for the mast and man, a size No. 8 bristle for the sky and a size No. 4 bristle for the yacht.

Fig. 25 (overleaf) is also painted on oil primed canvas with oil colour. It is 18 × 20cm (7 × 8in) and again uses

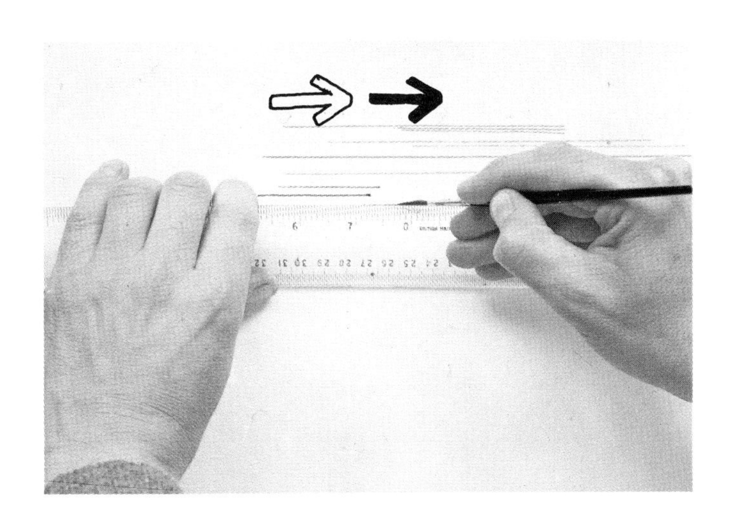

Use this method to paint rigging lines or any straight edges in watercolour or acrylic colour. If you are using oil colour, where the paint is wet, rest the ruler on the edge of the canvas. You can use wood but I prefer a transparent ruler so I can see where I am on the painting. The secret is to let the *ferrule* on the brush run against the *edge* of the ruler. Work from left to right if you are right-handed, and vice versa. *Hold your breath* and make the brush stroke.

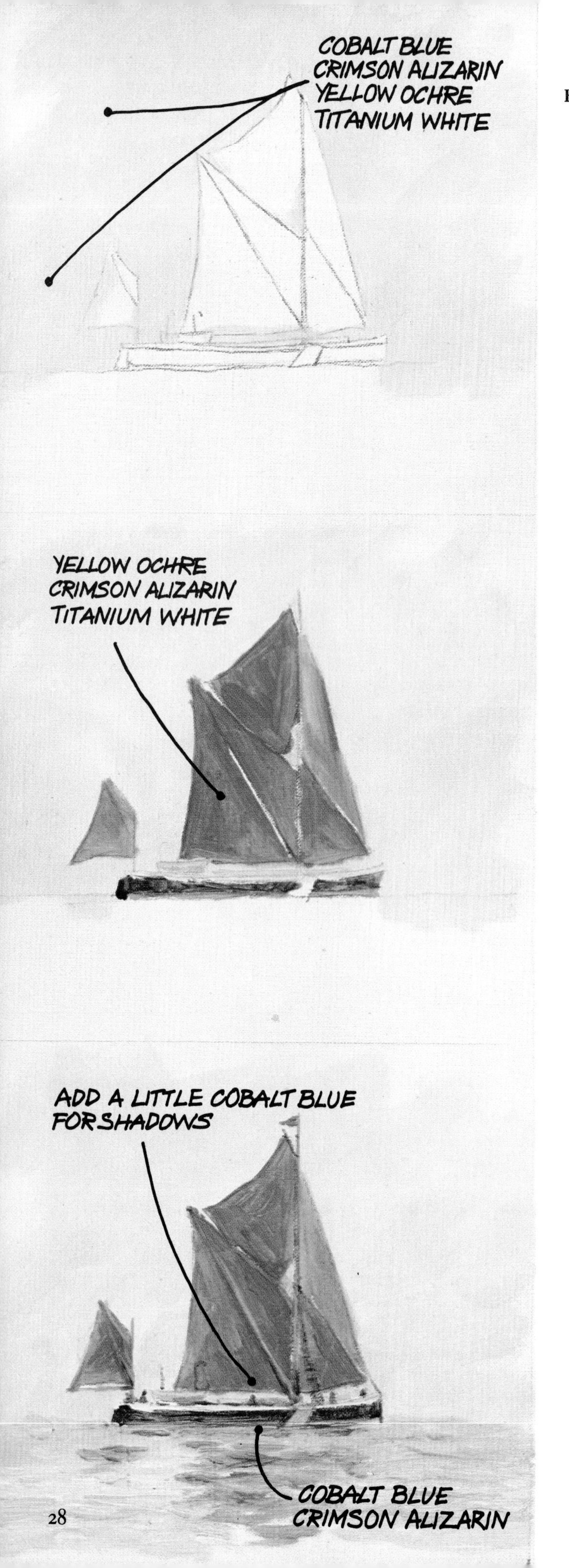

Fig. 25

only three colours. Note that the red is Crimson Alizarin, not Cadmium Red. This Thames barge is a little more ambitious than the previous exercises, but if you have coped with them you should manage this without much bother. I left the rigging off the barge to make it simpler and I haven't painted much detail. Use your size No. 8 bristle brush and start with the blue sky, working down to the horizon. Paint the sails and barge hull with your size No. 4 bristle brush. Next paint the water, reflections and the darker areas on the sails. Finally, darken the hull and put in any detail with your size No. 6 sable.

In the next exercise (**fig. 26**) I used three acrylic colours plus White and worked to a size of 18 × 20cm (7 × 8in). I have left the dark grey Ingres paper to represent the water, as we did in the water exercise in which we used white paper for water and added our reflections. The only difference is the paper colour, which is ideal for this wintry estuary scene. You should not find these boats too difficult, having done the previous exercises.

First paint the sky and land to the water's edge, using a size No. 6 nylon brush. Use the sky colours for the land, but with much less White. Next paint the smaller brown boat with a size No. 6 sable, and the white boat with a size No. 4 nylon brush. If you find the size No. 6 is a little too large for getting the detail try a smaller brush – sizes Nos. 3 or 4. As I have said, equipment is a very personal choice and I can only guide you. Paint the nearest boat using your size No. 6 sable brush, then paint the 'grey' snow on the two brown boats and the mast and shadow on the white boat. Paint the other side of the estuary with your size No. 6 sable brush, using dark colours first and adding light colours to represent the snow. The detail is suggested and painted very freely. Use your size No. 6 nylon brush to paint the mud and snow in the foreground. Add the snow highlights on the boats and mud, and any detail. If you want the paint to work more easily on this paper, add a little gel retarder to your paint.

Fig. 27 has a little more work in it. I painted it in acrylic colour on an Ingres paper while my brushes were still wet from the last one! Use your size No. 6 nylon brush throughout, except for detail work. I kept the yacht's hull simple in form and the shading very 'flat' (hardly any shading), with little moulding together of the colours. Don't try to copy the water exactly from mine but use my painting as a guide. Notice how the paper has been left to represent the sky this time, not the water. This exercise is the same size as the previous one.

If you can do this exercise with confidence and are happy with the results, you have come a long way and have reached a turning point. You should be relaxed and not worried about your work by now. If you are worried, don't be! Go back to the earlier exercises and practise more. 'Practise' simply means to paint. Paint more and more and you will get better and better and enjoy it more and more!

We are now going to use pen and pastel together. This exercise (**fig. 28**, overleaf) was done on an Ingres paper

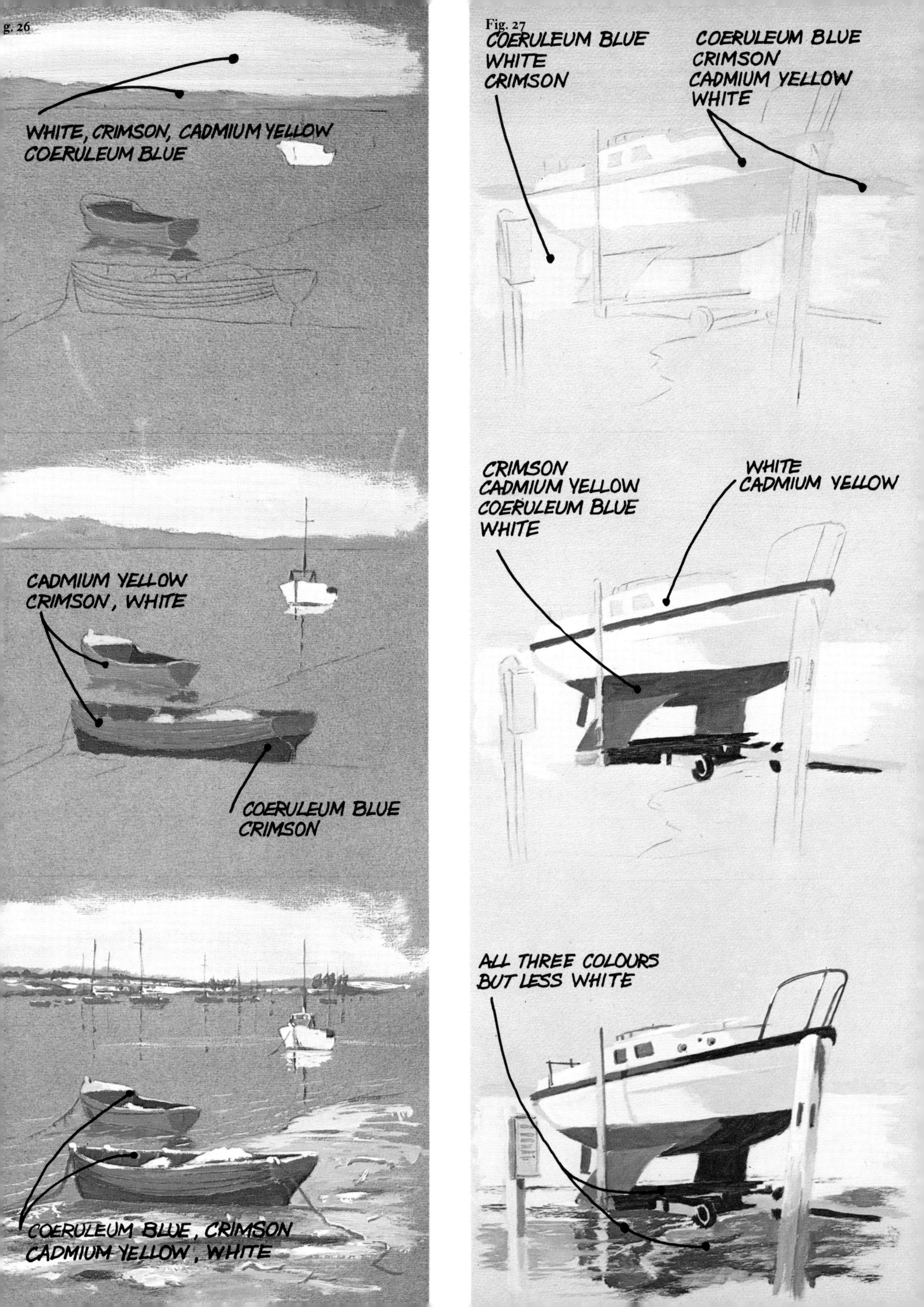
g. 26
WHITE, CRIMSON, CADMIUM YELLOW
COERULEUM BLUE
CADMIUM YELLOW
CRIMSON, WHITE
COERULEUM BLUE
CRIMSON
COERULEUM BLUE, CRIMSON
CADMIUM YELLOW, WHITE
Fig. 27
COERULEUM BLUE
WHITE
CRIMSON
COERULEUM BLUE
CRIMSON
CADMIUM YELLOW
WHITE
CRIMSON
CADMIUM YELLOW
COERULEUM BLUE
WHITE
WHITE
CADMIUM YELLOW
ALL THREE COLOURS
BUT LESS WHITE

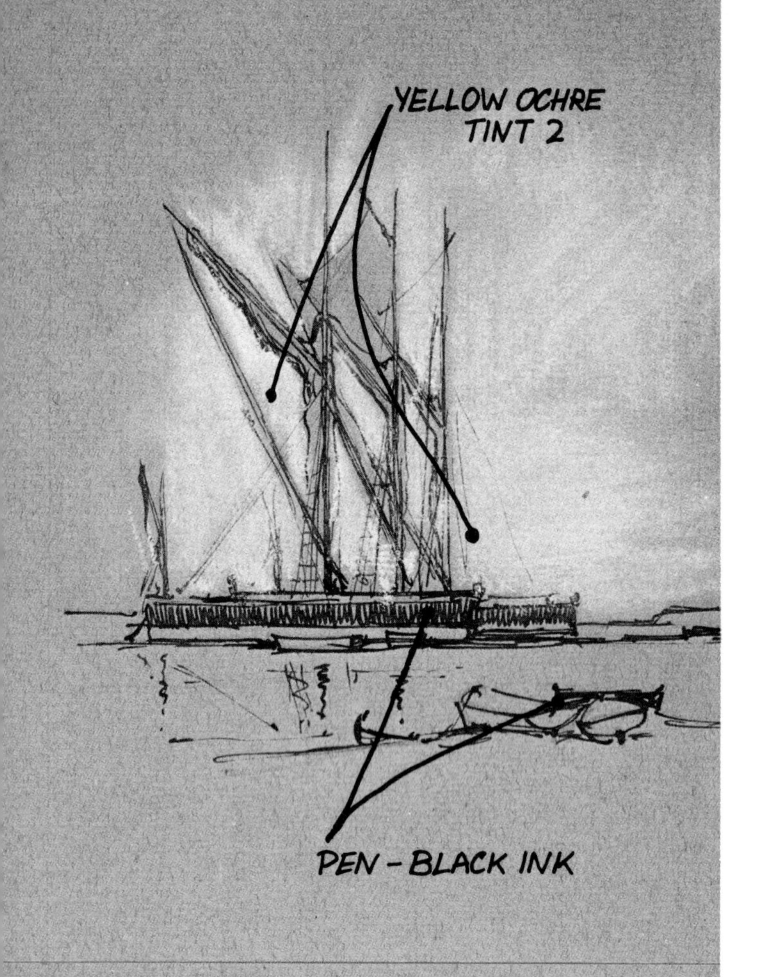

Fig. 28

Fig. 29

using a fountain pen with black ink and three pastel colours. It is not very large – 17 × 14cm (6½ × 5½in). Draw the barges and small boats with an HB pencil. You don't need detail – just the bare minimum for you to follow with a pen, which is the next step. The pen is suggested detail, so don't try to get everything spot on. We are after only an impression of rigging, masts and sails. If you were drawing the barges from a distance you would not be able to make out exactly what happens to the rigging; you would see only shapes. Therefore, only suggest the detail.

Next, paint the sky with Yellow Ochre Tint 2, leaving the sail area unpainted, and smudge it in with your finger. Paint the sails and their reflections with Burnt Umber Tint 4. Use Cadmium Red Tint 4 to paint the bottoms of the barges. Paint the sea behind the barges with Yellow Ochre Tint 2. The pastel will have covered some of your pen work, but don't worry about this. Brush off the excess pastel with a small, damp sable brush and your pen line will show again. Leave some pen covered as this will add to the character of your painting. Finish off with the pen, putting in any more detail you feel is necessary.

The final boat exercise (**fig. 29**) is perhaps the most complicated one. If you look at it you can see that the painting is simplified and the detail is suggested by a pen, with black ink. This technique is called pen and wash. It doesn't matter whether you use the pen before or after the paint. In this case, watercolour is used first, over an HB pencil drawing. I used GREENS RWS 140lb NOT SURFACE watercolour paper, size 14 × 32cm (5½ × 12½in). Paint the sky with your size No. 10 sable brush and Coeruleum Blue, Yellow Ochre and Crimson Alizarin mixed with plenty of water. Then paint the background building shapes with your size No. 6 sable brush and a mixture of French Ultramarine, Crimson Alizarin and Yellow Ochre. Next paint the dock side with Payne's Grey, Yellow Ochre and Crimson Alizarin. Then paint the deck with Yellow Ochre, and the hull and smoke stack with Payne's Grey, French Ultramarine and Yellow Ochre.

Put some detail on the superstructure with your size No. 6 sable brush and whatever dark colours you happen to have already mixed. Darken the hull with the same colours you used before, but use more paint. Use Coeruleum Blue, Crimson Alizarin and Yellow Ochre for the water. Paint the barge with Payne's Grey and Crimson Alizarin. When all the paint has dried, work over it with a pen. You can suggest as much or as little detail as you want.

When you are painting boats, don't let the 'technical correctness' bother you too much. If you were painting a detailed, close-up view of a boat or ship, then you would have to be technically correct for your painting to look right. However, if you were painting an impression of the same boat, your painting would show what you saw, in shape and form, which would not necessarily be technically correct. You are painting a picture – if the picture looks right you have created something successful, even if your boat sinks!

HARBOUR BRIC-A-BRAC

The harbour is usually the background for a boat picture, but it can play a very important part. Next time you are in a harbour make a point of sketching what I call bric-a-brac – the detail and close-ups of harbour fixtures and fittings. You will be able to use these sketches, especially information sketches, when you are painting at home.

Most objects at a harbour are related to boats – anchors, fishing nets etc. – but some are not so obvious. For instance, I once saw a dustbin standing proudly at the entrance to one yacht basin, yet if I had not noticed it particularly I would never have thought of putting it into a painting. The same applies to the petrol pumps in the sketches opposite. Until you 'see', you don't realize that what appears at first to be an unrelated object is in fact part and parcel of a harbour scene.

Naturally, each type of harbour has its own character. For instance, a fishing harbour has fishing nets, lobster pots, a predominance of seagulls and, if a boat has just docked with its catch, screaming seagulls! A yachting basin has a different atmosphere. Usually the activity is for pleasure as much as work and, of course, you can paint lots of yachts. Docks are different again, as they are dealing with cargo from large ships. Unfortunately, they are not an easy subject for the average person to find, as there are not many docks around the coasts. If you can paint in 'dockland', you can get tremendous pleasure from it, especially if you like your subject matter to be large. You will be in your element with the large cargo ships, cranes and warehouses.

The sketches opposite and below are just a tiny portion of all the various harbour bric-a-brac I have seen and sketched. Try to make a habit of looking around and making an information sketch of part of the harbour every time you finish a sketch or painting on location. It may take only 10 minutes, depending on the subject, and it will discipline you not to focus all your attention on the boats.

Always ask permission if you are in a harbour and are not sure if you can paint from a certain spot. Nine times out of ten you will be told to go ahead. If you had started work and then been told you should not be working there it would be embarrassing and a waste of time.

PAINTING FROM PHOTOGRAPHS

I believe in the use of photographs by students and professional artists. However, you *must* remember that: *photographs can never take the place of working directly from nature, or be a short cut to your own personal observation and experience of painting out-of-doors.*

Artists use electric light, squeeze paint from tubes, use plastic palettes and mixing dishes, work with nylon brushes and use, and accept, acrylic colours without thinking twice. It surprises me that these items all come through modern technology, yet people are not as afraid of them as they are of the camera. Perhaps, though, despite this trend to scorn it, many artists do use the camera. If you look at it objectively it is an aid to painting that can't be dismissed. Imagine asking John Constable, when he was out sketching: 'How would you like to take back that scene and look at it at any time on your own studio wall?' I think that situation speaks for itself.

Once we have accepted that the camera can be used as an aid – a working tool for the artist – we have to look at the way in which we use it. You could buy a very complicated camera and need a course of instruction to be able to use it correctly. You would then need years of experience to be able to use it for perfect results, but by then you would be a good photographer and have forgotten all about painting! You must concentrate on painting, not the camera. Use a simple camera that almost does the work for you. I use a 35mm camera, but any type is perfectly adequate for this purpose. All you want is a snapshot for reference. These are my ways of using photographs, but you may well develop your own methods.

You should always take your own photographs, so you will have experienced the scene with all your senses. This is very important, because when you see the photograph at home it will trigger off your memory banks. You will be back in the photograph, with all the smell and warmth of the scene. You will even remember that after taking the photograph you stepped back into a large mud puddle and got a black look from your partner! I don't think I am exaggerating this point, because it is important that the photograph helps to make you remember. You should take slides rather than prints, so you can project the image any size you like, sit in front of it and get into the mood. It is very difficult to get back the mood of an occasion by looking at a small print. Also, the larger you project the image the more detail you can see, and for painting boats this is very, very important.

I take photographs for information and atmosphere. When sketching, I find a spot, take a photograph and then forget about the camera. I know I will be able to see the scene again when the film has been developed. I paint the picture from my sketching notes. When the photographs come back I can check detail, and add or subtract if necessary. If the painting has a lot of complicated detail, or I am recording a special occasion, I will not start the finished painting until I have the photographs. If you treat your photographs this way, you will not be copying; you will be using them as memory triggers and for detail reference. Remember, photographs are for reference only: *you are creating your own experience on canvas, not the camera's.*

If you photograph from your sketching position, you will notice quite a difference between your sketch and the photograph, in the middle-distance and the distance. The distant images will look further away on the photograph than in your sketch, and those in the middle-distance tend to do the same. Apart from the technical reasons, I think this occurs because the camera sees everything, but *you see only what you want to see.* (This is why every artist's picture is different, even when painted of the same view.)

The photograph (**fig. 30**) was taken before I made the sketch. The inset photograph is me sketching the scene. You can see the point about the middle-distance appearing further away in a photograph. Look at the sketch (**fig. 31**) and you can see that the inn across the river looks closer than in the photograph, and that the trees play a more important part in the sketch. These are typical of the sketches and photographs from which I would paint a larger picture. I would use the proportions and composition (design) from the sketch and use the photograph for reference and as an aid to the main 'local' colours.

I asked an old boatman about the little boat. The man in the red jumper turned out to be an eel catcher. The net in the boat was an eel trap and the man set the traps at night. This explained the old oil lamp on the mast; I had not been able to work out its purpose. The man in the dinghy on the left in my sketch is the eel man going off for his lunch. Yes, I have put the same man in my sketch twice!

Students often ask me in a very quiet voice: 'Can I use photographs?', looking around quickly to see if their colleagues have heard. This confusion about the use of photographs should be dispelled once and for all. There is no crime in using them, as long as you use them correctly and are never afraid to say: 'Yes, I use photographs.'

Fig. 30 My photograph of the eel man and (inset) me sketching

Fig. 31 Pencil sketch of the eel man, 29 × 42cm (11½ × 16½in)

PAINTING FROM MEMORY

I am sure everyone at some time or another has painted from memory or imagination. Even when we were as young as three, we were given coloured pencils to draw with. We drew trees, boats, the sea, birds and so on. None of these subjects was in view at the time, so these early childhood drawings came from our memories. I believe working from memory is a natural way to paint or draw. We all find ourselves doodling while we are on the phone or listening to people in a meeting, and those doodles can be anything from scribbled lines to little drawings.

We cannot draw from memory without having seen an object first. We go out to sketch from nature in order to observe and collect information, and that information will also be in our memory banks for use at home when we want to paint from memory.

Imagination, though, is different. If you were asked to paint a boat from another world (as artists who illustrate science fiction books do) this would have to come from your imagination. Therefore, you need your memory for information, and your imagination to help you to create and add spice to your picture. Some people have better visual memories than others. If you find it difficult to remember scenes you have seen, try to cultivate your visual memory. I believe sketching is one of the best ways to do this. Sketching will teach you to observe, to 'look' and 'see', as we normally see only what we want to see.

If you simply looked at a harbour scene for ten minutes and walked away, the chances are you would remember only the obvious, the things you wanted to see – the restaurant on the other side of the harbour wall and the shop next to the car park where your car is. You might miss the big, red boat in front of you because it was in your way and you had to move to one side of it to see where the children had gone. You were interested in these things, and your visual memory was blind to the rest of the harbour. If you were interested in drawing the harbour at home later you would look at it with a completely different eye. You would see what you wanted to see – a picture. Next time you are out try to be aware of places as paintings. Naturally, the more you sketch the more you will be able to look at scenes as paintings and remember them.

This method of painting gives you complete control over your working conditions. You can decide what you are going to paint, the mood of nature you feel like painting and, of course, your working conditions at home. This is the ideal way of working in the winter when it may be difficult to get to the harbours. Unfortunately, nothing is ever perfect and we have a slight restriction when painting like this – getting accurate detail. Landscapes would be easier to paint this way than boat scenes. For instance, if a tree branch were drawn too high or too low, no one would be able to tell, but a wrongly positioned or angled mast on a yacht would be immediately evident. The amount of detail in a harbour scene is just too much to be able to recreate from memory, even with the help of imagination.

There are two ways round this. The first is to use existing sketches as a reference for the detail. You would then be using your memory to create your picture (the location), adding more information from your sketches, and using your imagination to add a little spice. You can also get detail from photographs you have taken.

The alternative is to paint your picture without any close-up detail work. Let your nearest boat or building be too far away (middle-distance onwards) to need close detail work. You will then concentrate on the atmosphere of the picture. Your sky will be very important and your foreground can be of a general nature, such as water or mud banks.

If you read that again carefully you will see that you have the sky, the empty foreground, and boats or buildings in the middle-distance. The sky gives you the same licence as a tree can in landscape (when painting from memory) because a cloud can be a little too thick, long, short or dark and it will not show. The foreground, empty of 'close-up' boats or bric-a-brac and consisting of water and mud, also gives you plenty of licence to be able to represent it on paper from memory. Finally, the boats and buildings would not need much detail because they would be in the middle-distance. Sunsets and early morning paintings are absolutely perfect for this because your boats are silhouetted against the sky. If you remember, I said earlier that you can't see detail in silhouettes.

Let me now explain how I prepare to paint a finished painting (not an experiment or an exercise) from memory. You will probably adapt your own way, but naturally that doesn't matter, as long as you enjoy your painting.

I draw the proportions to which I am going to do the finished painting on my sketch-pad. Usually I try to work to half the size of the finished painting. I sit in front of the canvas or paper on which I am going to paint. This is important as it gives me the real size to which I will be working. I then relax and imagine different moods of nature. These come from different days I have been out – not necessarily painting. Our memory banks are full of these visions and, depending on the mood you are in, one will come to the surface. If you find it difficult, look at some of your sketches or family photographs. These could easily trigger off a memory of mood and atmosphere. The scene you call up depends very much on the mood you are in. A good day's work behind you, or a rough time with the boss or the children will make different memories come to the front. A good day is likely to bring forth peaceful memories and a not so good day may release visions of

My pencil sketch, drawn from my memory and imagination, 9 × 20cm (3½ × 7¾in), and the painting into which it developed, 18 × 39cm (7 × 15½in), watercolour and pen

rough sea, windswept harbours, and so on.

When you have this vision in your mind you are ready to start the sketch. Capturing a mood of nature in a painting gives it life, whichever style you paint in, and without this a painting is dead. The next stage is to decide on the content of the picture. This could easily come from the scene that gave you the mood. If not, think of the mood you have chosen and create a picture around it. If your mood is that of a windy, rainy day, you must go for dramatic lines and shapes to give movement, perhaps a yacht with the sails billowing out or an inland waterway with the wind scurrying across the water and storm clouds coming up. You must practise this – it is something you can cultivate, but you will be practising and getting better all your life.

Finally, I draw the sketch on paper, not on the canvas or paper I am to use for the painting, so that it is never covered up and is always there to refer to. If your picture changes course from your sketch, don't worry – remember, you are creating it and you can create it any way you want. This method of painting gives you total control over your subject and painting conditions. I love to paint this way. You won't be disappointed when you try it.

NOTES ON SKETCHING OUT-OF-DOORS

Before we start on the stage-by-stage exercises, we must consider the reasons for and the requirements of sketching out-of-doors. First of all, it is necessary to work from nature to understand it. Boats and harbours are only found under the sky, not indoors. This doesn't mean you can only do your painting outside. On the contrary, I do many paintings indoors, but the information and inspiration comes from sketching on location. You may find it difficult to go out sketching as much as you would like to. In this case, do as much work as possible when the occasion arises. You can save time by doing small sketches. If you are happy with painting in colour from pencil sketches, then do more pencil sketches on location. They can be done far more quickly than a painting. On a time basis, pencil sketches give you more information than an *information sketch* done in paint. On the other hand, you can get more out of an *atmosphere sketch* done in colour than in pencil. Sketching habits are personal – you have your own requirements and restrictions. I can guide you, but you should then let your circumstances dictate the methods and ways of your sketching trips. Always carry a sketch-book and pencil with you, especially when you go on holiday, and if anyone objects, tell them it was my idea!

Fig. 32 is an information sketch done with a 2B pencil. It is 29 × 42cm (11½ × 16½in). The photographs show the scene and me working. **Fig. 33** is another page in my sketch-book and is the same size. I had sketched as much information as I could see. The old barge at the top of the sketch is the first exercise you will be doing. (I have painted this barge many times in different moods.)

Let us look at the requirements for sketching out-of-doors. The most important one, other than your materials, is clothing. You must have enough to be comfortable and warm. This is not being soft (I hope I am not showing my age!) – when you are sitting still for a few hours even in moderate weather you can get cold. Always take more

Fig. 32 Pencil information sketch, 29 × 42cm (11½ × 16½in)

Fig. 33 Pencil information sketch, 29 × 42cm (11½ × 16½in)

clothing than you think you need. You can always take some off, but you can't put on what you haven't brought. You may want to take a folding stool or chair with you, or take a chance on being able to paint a scene where you can find somewhere to sit, such as a harbour wall or beach. You must be comfortable when you are working. I know this is almost impossible some times because of the view you want to draw, but you can only give your best to your work when you are relaxed and in a comfortable position.

The next hurdle is to decide what you are going to sketch. The following point is important and one I have learnt from bitter experience. When you find a scene you automatically say to yourself: 'That's for me ... or would it be better on the other side of that blue boat?' When you walk to that spot you hesitate again, and walk to the next spot. In the end you have wasted all your sketching time jumping around looking for that 'better' spot. There is nothing wrong with this; in fact, it can show tremendous enthusiasm, but it does not get any work on paper. This has happened to me on quite a few occasions and, although I have soaked in the atmosphere, I have nothing on paper to show for it. To stop this happening you must discipline yourself to draw or paint the first scene that inspires you, and then walk around and find the next.

Once you have chosen the scene it can be difficult to decide where to position the scene on your paper – where to start and where to stop. An excellent way of doing this is to cut a mask out of paper or thin card with an opening of

My photograph of the scene sketched in **fig. 32**, and me sketching

about 10 × 15cm (4 × 6in). Make the shape the same proportion as your sketch-book. Hold the mask up at arm's length, close one eye and move your hand backwards and forwards and side to side, until the scene is sitting happily in the opening (see **fig. 34**). Make mental notes of the positions of the scene's main features where they 'hit' the edges of the mask, and then draw these 'key' features on your sketch-pad.

Sketching materials are largely determined by the medium in which you like to work. Pencil, pastel and watercolour equipment are more easily carried than that for oil or acrylic colour. If you know you are going to paint near your car there is no problem about carrying equipment. If, however, you are going to roam about looking for a spot then you can take only a limited amount of gear. If, for instance, you want to do a day's oil painting, using an easel and all the necessary equipment, I suggest you find a spot before you set off with your 'portable studio'. Even the lightest equipment gets heavy after half an hour's trekking, especially if you are walking on a pebbled beach. Remember to carry your sketch-book in polythene – there is usually too much water about. I dropped mine only once before I learned my lesson!

If you are not used to going out sketching, I suggest you start off by pencil sketching. All you need is an HB and a 2B or 3B pencil. Sharpen them as I have shown in **fig. 35**, with enough lead showing and a long, gradual taper to the lead, allowing you to see the pencil point easily when working. Also in **fig. 35**, I have shaded with HB, 2B and 6B pencils, to show the different tones you can get. HB is the hardest pencil and 6B is the softest (the blackest). There are four pencils in between – from 2B to 5B. Cartridge paper is ideal for pencil sketching and you can buy all sizes of cartridge paper sketching-pads. Always have a putty rubber with you. So, all the equipment you need to start sketching is one or two pencils, a sketch-pad and a putty rubber.

When you are ready to go out and paint, watercolour is the most convenient medium and is easy to carry. You will need a watercolour box, a watercolour sketch-pad (these usually contain watercolour paper – but you can use cartridge paper), two watercolour brushes, sizes Nos. 6 and 10, and a water holder. An easel is optional. I don't use one for watercolour unless I am working on a painting larger than 38 × 51cm (15 × 20in).

There is one problem with watercolour. It has a mind all of its own and unforeseen things sometimes happen. There are ways of rescuing a watercolour if it does get out of hand, and you haven't time to start again. Mix White Designer's Gouache colour with your watercolours. It will make them opaque and you can go over areas you don't like and correct them. An alternative is to draw over your painting with a pen using black waterproof drawing ink, a felt-tip pen or a fountain pen, turning it into a pen and wash drawing. This method will usually salvage a poor watercolour and make it a good painting, and I have done this on many occasions.

Remember that your model does not come home with you! When you leave the harbour all your information is in your sketch. If you feel it necessary, put written notes on your pencil sketches, but not on watercolour sketches, as these could quite easily be framed and hung as 'paintings'. The more watercolour sketching you do, the more your sketches will turn into paintings in their own right, but continue to use them as information sketches.

For normal sketching, oil and acrylic colour call for more equipment and are not so easy to carry around. If you plan to paint a particular place, and are going to be there most of the day, then the carrying will be only to get there and back. You can't walk around with a lot of equipment, looking for spots, setting everything up for an hour, and moving on again. It would become too tiring and the fun and enjoyment would go out of it. I have made a point of this earlier but it is important. Make sketching a happy day, with that added satisfaction of having created something new and having given yourself plenty of new information

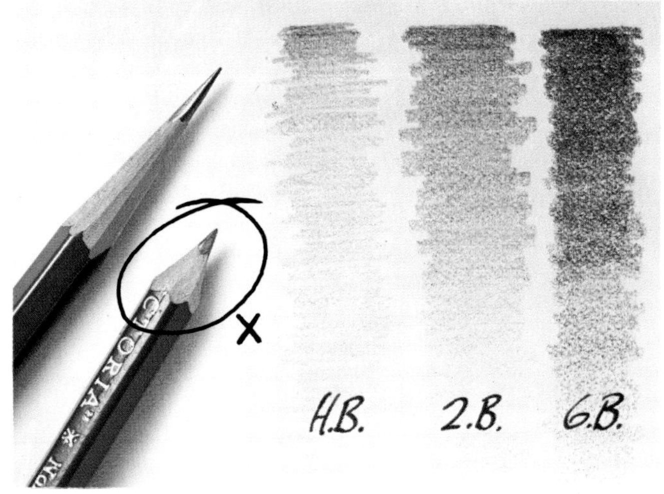

Fig. 35

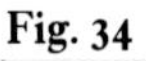
Fig. 34

These sketches are shown half the size they were done

Here I am working on *Three Boats*, and my photograph of the scene itself

from which to work.

When you are sketching boats and harbours you must pay attention to the usual do's and don'ts, as in the countryside. Be careful that you don't get caught by an incoming tide. If you are not sure about the tides, ask. You can set up and start work and then find the tide has moved so fast that you have to move before you are finished, and it can be dangerous. If you want to sketch in a busy harbour, make sure you are not going to be in anybody's way. Always ask permission if you want to work somewhere which looks 'private'. If you are going to an estuary take your wellies – you will more than likely need them. Finally, enjoy yourself and soak up the atmosphere!

Three Boats, 39 × 56cm (15½ × 22in). Watercolour information sketch. This took three hours and is the type of sketch I am pleased to use as a painting in its own right

Brixham Harbour, Devon, 37 × 53cm ($14\frac{1}{2}$ × 21in). Watercolour information sketch. I did not use a pen for the detail on this, and am very happy with the result, although at first I did not think I could manage this without a pen

Photograph of the scene at Brixham Harbour

Detail of *Brixham Harbour, Devon*

EXERCISE ONE
PENCIL SKETCH
ON LOCATION

In the following pages I have taken six subjects and worked each one through its progressive stages for you to follow and copy. I have tried to give you a brush-by-brush account of how I worked on each subject. Naturally, it is impossible to discuss *every* brush stroke – we would need a book this size for just one exercise – but I have analyzed each stage and explained the important features and how to paint them. I talked into a tape recorder, explaining what I was doing as I painted each exercise. I had to decide where to stop painting and have each stage photographed. It was a daunting task, but very worthwhile. This method enables you to see the *same painting* through its stages of development so that you can compare any stage with what was done earlier.

It is also important to know the size of the painting (not of the reproduction) to give you a relative scale to which to adjust. The actual size is indicated next to the finished stage. The close-up illustrations for each exercise are reproduced the same size as I painted them. This gives you the chance to see the actual brush or pencil strokes and the detail that was put in. Finally, I have illustrated the method used for a particular part of the painting that I think you need to see more closely.

I have painted these subjects in my own style which has evolved over the years. The way I paint in this book is the way I work; I haven't made the paintings work for the book. We all have a creative style of our own and this will come out naturally. Once you have mastered the medium, *let your own style come to the fore.*

In this first exercise I have tried to recreate a normal sequence of events; going on location, preparing a pencil sketch (information sketch) and using this sketch to work from at home. We will work from this sketch in watercolour in exercise two. I photographed the old, disused barge at Topsham, Devon, to show you what artist's licence I took with the sketch and the watercolour.

First stage Position the distant hills, the old barge and the distinct mud line below the barge on your paper with your 2B pencil. Then draw the shape of the barge but don't put in any detail.

Second stage Work on the barge, putting in the shadows, with shading, to create form. Start with the superstructure and work down to the hull. Practise shading with your 2B pencil on scraps of paper to get used to the tonal range of the pencil (see **fig. 35**, page 40). Put in the edge of the reeds, working your pencil up and down to produce dark and light strokes. Put in the rails on the barge and a little detail.

Finished stage Work on the wet mud, shade in the reflection and put in detail on the barge and the rest of the sketch. I have sketched this boat, several times (**fig. 33**, page 39 is my sketch made on location). The character of the boat, mud and water always excites me.

First stage

Second stage

Finished stage
23 × 36cm
(9 × 14in)

EXERCISE TWO
PAINTING AT HOME FROM PENCIL SKETCH
IN WATERCOLOUR

Let's start painting! Because this is the first proper exercise in colour, you may be tight and not relaxed. This is quite natural, I feel the same way when I start a special painting. Try to relax and I will help you through. Read each stage through and understand it before you start. If you prefer to try another medium first, start with another exercise.

In this exercise, and all the others that follow, it is important to know that when you are mixing colours, the colour you should mix into is the one I mention first: add the other colours (in smaller amounts) to this one. The first colour usually represents the main colour. White is usually last unless, of course, it is the main colour. Sets of oil or acrylic colours are shown at the beginning of some exercises. They comprise only the main primary colours or mixed colours used for particular areas.

As you have drawn the sketch of the barge in the previous exercise you will be familiar with your first painting subject, which will help you to relax a bit more. I did this painting on GREENS RWS 140lb NOT SURFACE watercolour paper. Off you go and good luck!

First stage Draw the picture with your HB pencil. Wet the paper from the top, down to the barge, with your size No. 10 sable brush. Mix Coeruleum Blue and Crimson Alizarin with plenty of water and work down the sky, adding Yellow Ochre and Hooker's Green No. 1 as you paint the hills and each side of the barge.

Second stage Once the first stage has dried, paint the distant hills with your size No. 10 sable brush and a mix of Payne's Grey, Crimson Alizarin and Yellow Ochre. Work from left to right with horizontal brush strokes. As you progress downwards, add a little Hooker's Green No. 1 to your colours. When the paint is nearly dry, add a wash of Yellow Ochre, Crimson Alizarin and a little Hooker's Green No. 1 to represent the reeds. Let this wash overlap slightly with the last area you have painted. This darkens the tone and gives more depth to that area.

Third stage Make sure the paint around the barge has dried. Paint the cabin with your size No. 6 sable brush and Crimson Alizarin, Yellow Ochre and a touch of French Ultramarine. Paint both sides of the cabin, leaving two holes for the windows. Work around the rails, leaving paper showing. Use a weak wash of Yellow Ochre to paint the deck up to the bows. Paint the dark area in front of the cabin, where there isn't any deck, with Payne's Grey and Yellow Ochre. Use the same colours for the rails and shadow behind the cabin. Paint the hull, starting from the stern and working along the light-coloured area, with a mix of Yellow Ochre, Crimson Alizarin and a little Payne's Grey. Use plenty of water, except for the rusty parts, to keep most of this area white. Work down the next section of the barge with Payne's Grey, Yellow Ochre and Crimson Alizarin. Make the area under the stern darker by using less water with your colours. Suggest the tops of the reeds growing in front of the barge by working your brush point in downwards strokes. Use the same colours, with less water, for the darkest part of the hull. Paint up to the reeds as you did in the previous section of the barge. Next put a shadow on the right-hand side of the cabin. Simply paint a wash of French Ultramarine and Crimson Alizarin over the original wash you have done earlier in this stage. (Don't forget to leave the windows and rails.) Suggest trees in the background with a mixture of French Ultramarine, Cadmium Yellow Pale and Crimson Alizarin. Do this freely – these are only impressions of trees. Finally, paint the front of the reeds with Crimson Alizarin, French Ultramarine and Yellow Ochre. Work the brush in vertical strokes, as you did with your pencil in exercise one. Make areas darker by using more paint and less water, and lighter by using less paint and more water. The reeds under the bows of the boat should be darker because they are in shadow.

First stage

Second stage

Third stage

Fourth stage

Fourth stage Start by painting the mud and water. Don't try to copy me exactly or the results will be disastrous. Use my method, but because of the very nature of the application your happy accidents will be different from mine. Start with your size No. 10 sable brush (use this for all the mud and water), saturated in clean water. Drag it over the area. Don't let the brush go everywhere – you are not trying to soak the paper, so let some remain dry. You will then get happy accidents of paint running into wet areas and mixing. Let the strokes with the wet brush follow the direction of the mud, in perspective. Paint the reflected blue area of water with Coeruleum Blue mixed with clean water. Paint the mud and water with Coeruleum Blue, Payne's Grey, Crimson Alizarin, Yellow Ochre and Hooker's Green No. 1. Work in broad strokes and change your colour mix as you go. Paint over the reeds on the right-hand side of the boat to add more shadow. When this has nearly dried, put in the reflection of the barge with your size No. 6 sable brush and a wash of Payne's Grey, Crimson Alizarin and Yellow Ochre. Use a wash of the same colours to represent the shadow of the barge on the mud and reeds to the right of it.

Finished stage By the time you reach this stage of a painting you will have various colours mixed on your palette – some light, some dark and some in between. I am sure you are now well able to select an appropriate colour to add the detail and crispness to your painting. Start with the barge. Use your size No. 6 sable brush and a dark colour to paint the cabin windows. Draw the planks on the shadow side of the cabin with the point of the brush. Paint the rails and ropes with a dark mix of Payne's Grey, Crimson Alizarin and Yellow Ochre. Paint a wash over the dark part of the hull, and on to the mud and right-hand

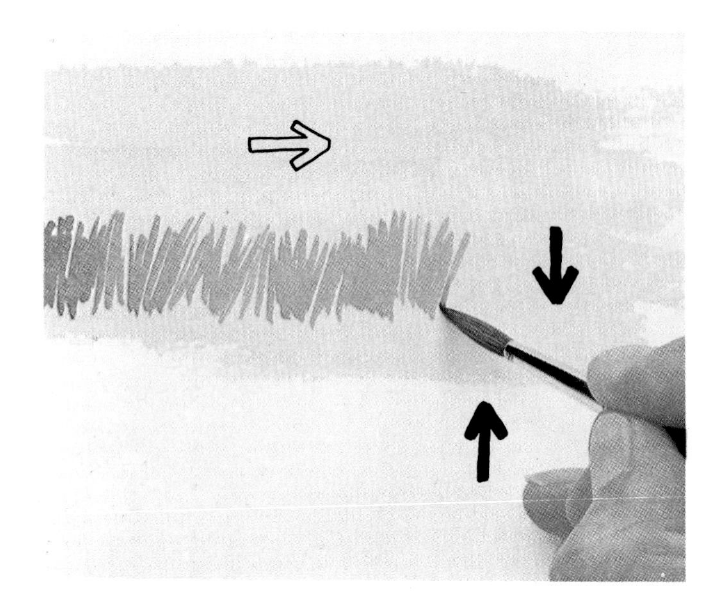

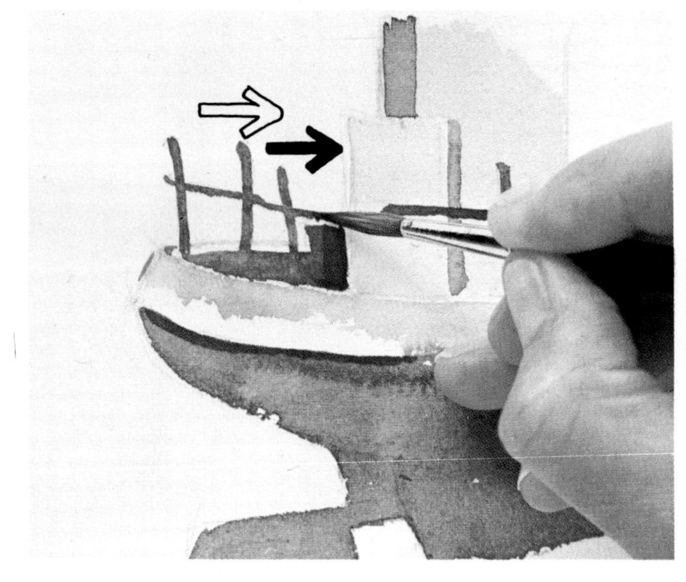

Finished stage 23 × 36cm (9 × 14in)

reeds to create shadows, using the original dark hull colours. Use the same colours to make the reflections darker. Finally, paint some line work on the mud with a strong colour. Try not to overwork a watercolour. Look at the fourth stage again – it would make a very pleasing watercolour just as it is.

EXERCISE THREE
FISHING BOAT
IN OIL COLOUR

First stage

Second stage

Third stage

I saw this fishing boat waiting to dock on the River Dart in Devon. It was late evening with a misty, watery sun going down. I chose oil colour and used a gel medium to dry the paint more quickly on the oil primed canvas. I sketched the boat on location and completed the painting in one sitting, without any acute problems of the paint being too wet to work over. I worked as directly as I could to avoid a lot of over-painting, which is my natural style. I didn't use a palette knife, but used the same brushes both to mix colours and to paint. I used a 50/50 mix of turpentine and linseed oil as my medium for mixing the paint, and turpentine for cleaning my brushes.

First stage Draw the picture with an HB pencil. Paint the 'sun area' with Cadmium Yellow, Yellow Ochre and Titanium White with a little Crimson Alizarin and your size No. 10 bristle brush. Work from the centre outwards and add Cobalt Blue to your mix. Work down the canvas with the same colours, using horizontal brush strokes for the water.

Second stage Paint the distant hills with your size No. 4 bristle brush and Cobalt Blue, Crimson Alizarin, Yellow Ochre and Titanium White. Start with the furthest hill and work forwards to the houses on the water's edge. Let the brush wander around, dabbing the canvas with light and dark colours, suggesting shapes of boats in the distance. Use the same colours to paint the suggested boats on the right of the fishing boat.

Third stage Start with your size No. 6 sable brush. Put in the masts of the fishing boat with Yellow Ochre and touches of Crimson Alizarin and Titanium White. Use the turpentine and linseed oil mix to dilute your paint and make it run off the brush easily. For the rigging use your Series 56, size No. 1 sable and ox brush. Paint the cabin with your size No. 4 bristle brush and Titanium White, Yellow Ochre and a touch of Crimson Alizarin. Add a little Cobalt Blue for the shadow areas. Put in detail work with your size No. 6 sable brush. Paint the inside of the hull, behind and in front of the cabin, with a dark colour. Change to your size No. 4 bristle brush and Cobalt Blue, Crimson Alizarin and Yellow Ochre to paint the dark band around the top of the hull. Paint the main part of the hull with Cobalt Blue and touches of Crimson Alizarin and Titanium White. Finish with the dark water-line band.

Finished stage Put in the reflections of the large fishing

Finished stage 41 × 30cm (16 × 12in)

boat with your size No. 4 bristle brush. Use the colours you used for the boat and work with horizontal brush strokes. Use your size No. 6 sable brush to paint the men. Use Cadmium Red and a touch of Yellow Ochre for the red one, and dark colours for the other two. Then paint their reflections. Paint the reflected light among the dark reflections with your size No. 4 bristle brush and light sky colours. This will make the water more 'watery'. Don't be afraid to use thick paint for these highlights. Finally, put in any more detail you feel is necessary.

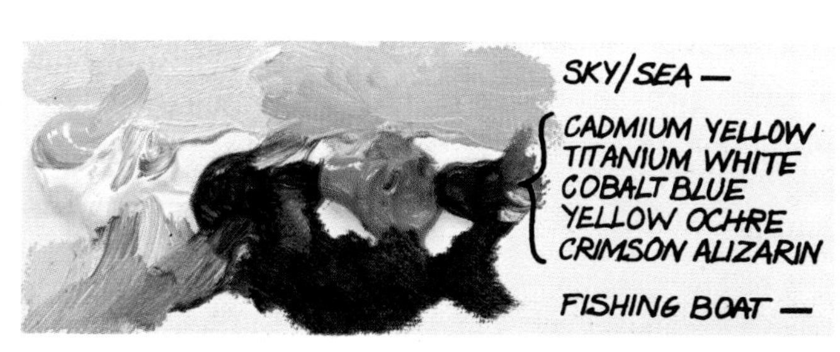

EXERCISE FOUR
THAMES BARGES
IN WATERCOLOUR AND PEN

I think most artists who like painting boats get excited about the old Thames barges. They are full of character and very distinctive with their dark hulls and brown sails. They have a tremendous amount of rigging lines for the masts and sails and this could be daunting to the student. Therefore, I have painted this exercise in watercolour and pen. I have used the pen mainly for the rigging, and this may help you to suggest it better than a brush. Watercolour and pen is a natural technique for painting boats where there are masts, sails and rigging. I have used a fountain pen filled with black Indian drawing ink, but a felt-tip pen, a mapping pen or even a sharpened match stick dipped in drawing ink work just as well. The aim is not to draw every line to perfection and put every rigging line in exactly the correct place, but to get atmosphere and feeling into the painting with a controlled freedom of brush and pen. Nothing is exact, the rigging may not be correct, but the impression is there and that is what to aim for – the impression of a couple of barges moored on a wet, muddy east coast estuary.

First stage I used GREENS RWS 140lb NOT SURFACE watercolour paper. Draw the picture with your HB pencil. Wet the paper with clean water, except the sail and hull areas of the two main barges, using your size No. 10 sable brush. Now load the brush really well with French Ultramarine, Crimson Alizarin, Yellow Ochre and plenty of water. Paint down from the top, subtly changing your colour mix as you go, over the mud to the bottom of your picture. Leave the horizon to the right of the barges unpainted – this will give distance to your picture. Let the paint dry before you go on to the second stage.

Second stage Paint the masts on the two foreground barges with a mix of Yellow Ochre and Crimson Alizarin, using your size No. 6 sable brush. Paint the hull of the nearest barge with Payne's Grey, Crimson Alizarin and a touch of Yellow Ochre. Use lighter paint (more water, less paint) for the end of the barge, and leave some white paper for suggested lettering and a line across the stern. Don't paint the lee-board. Use Cadmium Red with a little Burnt Umber for the red area, and paint it while the dark area is still wet. This will allow the colours to run into each other. Leave white paper for the mooring rope. Next paint the furthest of the barges in the foreground, using Coeruleum Blue for the blue area and the rowing boat at her stern. Use the hull colours from the first barge for the dark areas. Use Payne's Grey and Yellow Ochre for the shadow area of the white rowing boat and leave white paper for the lightest areas. Strengthen these colours to paint the shadow inside the rowing boat. Use Cadmium Yellow Pale and Crimson Alizarin for the sails on the two barges, adding Payne's Grey for the darker areas.

Third stage Paint the right-hand distant trees with your size No. 6 sable brush and a mix of French Ultramarine, Crimson Alizarin and Yellow Ochre. Leave white paper for the barge masts. Start on the left, loading your brush with plenty of water. Strengthen your paint as you work towards the right. Use the same colours for the left-hand trees. Give the impression of trees by painting in downwards strokes. Next wet the mud area below the barge, using *clean* water. Paint the reflections with your size No. 10 sable brush. Use the barge colours, but add a little Hooker's Green No. 1. Continue into the reflections of the sails, using the colours you used for the sails originally. You will be working on a wet area so your colours will run to give a water effect. Therefore, you will not be able to

First stage

Second stage

Third stage

Fourth stage

achieve exactly what I have done – your water reflections will find their own way on your painting. Paint the lee-board on the side of the hull, using the hull colours, lighter, and your size No. 6 sable brush. Use the same colours and brush to paint the inside of the white rowing boat again, and the dark area of the blue rowing boat. Paint over the hull again, with the same colours, to darken it. Paint the deck work, suggesting quite freely an impression of bits and pieces. Finally, put in some rigging lines and their reflections.

Fourth stage Paint the hulls of the distant barges with your size No. 6 sable brush and a wash of French Ultramarine, Crimson Alizarin and Yellow Ochre. Use horizontal brush strokes. Paint the mast and sails with a watery mix of the sail colours used for the nearer barges. Use these colours to put in the reflections on the mud. Paint the rowing boat on the right-hand side with Cadmium Red and Cadmium Yellow Pale. Suggest the boats on the left of the large barge, with French Ultramarine, Crimson Alizarin and Yellow Ochre. Put a darker line (wash) of paint on the bottom of the left-hand trees with these colours. Use Payne's Grey and Yellow Ochre to darken the inside of the right-hand rowing boat. Darken the sails on the nearest barge, repeating the original colours but making them darker (less water). Put a dark wash over the hull of the nearest barge and on to the mud, so the boat merges with the mud. Use Yellow Ochre to paint over the stern of the first barge, where it was left white, and the mooring rope and some rigging lines.

Finished stage This stage is done with a fountain pen and black drawing ink. Start on the nearest barge and draw over the masts, sails and rigging and work down the hull. It is up to you how much detail you put in. Work all over the painting, drawing with your pen and using my painting as a guide. Let the pen work freely and don't labour it. You are creating an impression, not a working drawing of a barge. I am sure that if my barges were to come alive, the mast and sails would fall down – but as a painting they stand up!

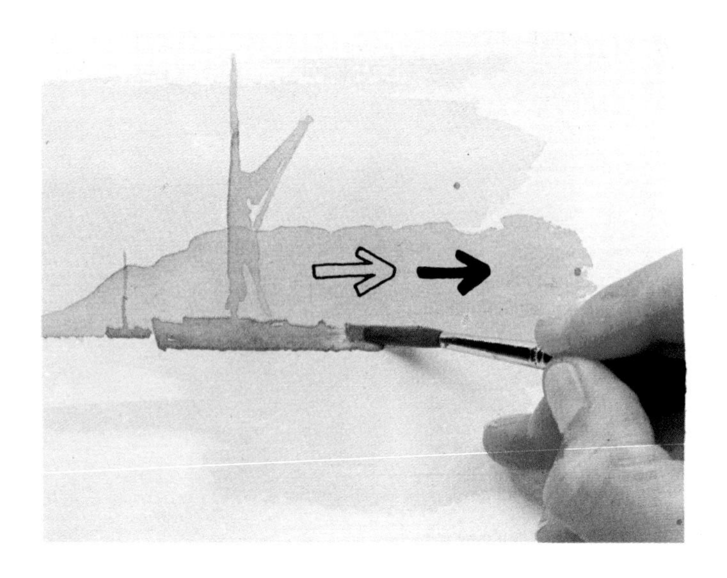

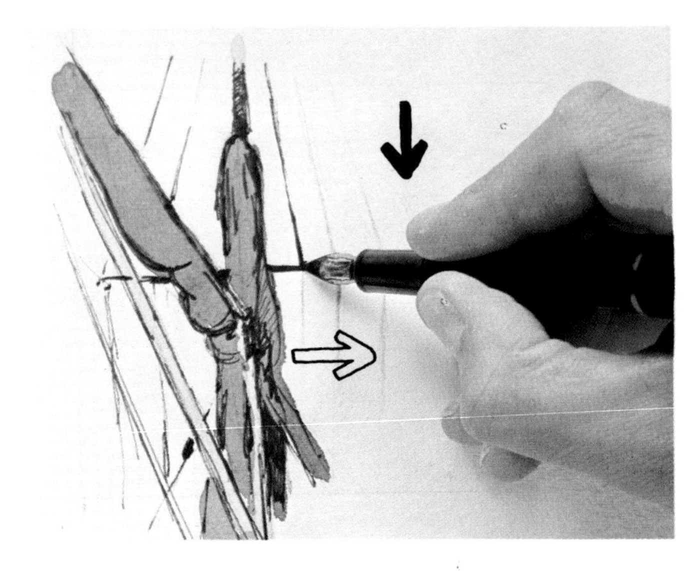

Finished stage 36 × 53cm (14 × 21in)

EXERCISE FIVE
QUEEN ELIZABETH 2
IN ACRYLIC COLOUR

First stage

Second stage

Third stage

I like this subject because of the majesty of the ocean liner *Queen Elizabeth 2*, gracefully gliding into harbour as the tugs rush around and mother her. I painted this on an acrylic primed canvas.

First stage Draw the picture with your HB pencil. Put in the sky with your size No. 12 nylon brush and Coeruleum Blue, Crimson, Cadmium Yellow and White. Start at the top and work down, darkening the colours as you approach the horizon. Use White and touches of Crimson and Cadmium Yellow for the high, fluffy clouds. Dab your brush across the sky to get this effect. Paint the light-coloured clouds on the right of the ship with a stronger mix of the same colours.

Second stage Paint the distant hills and harbour wall with your size No. 2 nylon brush and Coeruleum Blue, Crimson, Cadmium Yellow, Bright Green and White. Change your colours and tones constantly as you work from the top of the hills to the water's edge. Don't try to put in a lot of detail. Paint the sea with your size No. 6 nylon brush, using the sky colours. The ship has left some water still and oily looking. Paint this with wet, downwards strokes, as in **fig. 18**, page 24. Paint the rest of the water up to this area, using short, sharp, horizontal strokes. Keep changing the colours.

Third stage Start painting the *QE2* with your size No. 4 nylon brush. Paint the funnel and work down the left-hand side of the superstructure (the shadow side) first. Don't put in any detail. Use the sky colours for the shadow side, and primarily White for the sunlit side. Next paint the blue area of the hull, with Ultramarine, Crimson, Cadmium Yellow and a little White. Use Cadmium Red for the water-line. Now put in detail – windows and dark shadow lines – on the ship, using your size No. 6 sable and size No. 2 nylon brushes and a mix of Ultramarine and Crimson, keeping your paint watery. Paint the dark part of the funnel with the colours used for the blue hull. Paint the tugs in the same way. Use your size No. 2 nylon brush. Paint the shadow side of the white areas first, then the sunlit side and the dark hull. Note there is no 'worked' detail. Paint the left-hand tugs in darker tones as they are not catching sunlight. Paint a dark reflection under the ship with your size No. 6 sable brush with the hull colours and plenty of water and no White. Use these colours to paint some movement lines on the water, from the tugs and *QE2*.

Finished stage 41 × 30cm (16 × 12in)

Finished stage Put in the remaining detail with your size No. 6 sable brush. Start with the mast and work over the ship. Use light and dark colours to paint the yachts in the distance. Finally, with thick White and a little Cadmium Yellow, put in the white of the broken waves.

EXERCISE SIX
FERRY IN HARBOUR
IN ACRYLIC COLOUR

I am not sure if this ferry is still operating. I sketched it a few years ago at Gosport, Hampshire, when it was crossing to Portsmouth. In the distance, to the right of the funnel, you can see the masts of HMS *Victory*, Lord Nelson's flagship at the Battle of Trafalgar. The day was a bit chilly and I have shown a passing rain shower in the sky to help to create the atmosphere. This was painted on an acrylic primed canvas.

First stage Draw the picture with your HB pencil. Paint the sky with your size No. 12 nylon brush and Ultramarine, Crimson, Raw Umber and plenty of White. Use less White to paint the darker clouds. Go back over the light area to suggest dark clouds breaking away from the main bank. Work down into the darker area, adding a little Raw Sienna. Put in the sunlit clouds to the right of the dark ones, using White, Cadmium Yellow and Crimson.

SKY/WATER —
WHITE
ULTRAMARINE
CRIMSON
RAW UMBER
RAW SIENNA
CADMIUM YELLOW

GREEN OF FERRY —
WHITE
COERULEUM BLUE
CADMIUM YELLOW

DARK HULL OF FERRY —
ULTRAMARINE
CRIMSON
BURNT UMBER
WHITE

Second stage Paint the cranes with your size No. 6 sable brush and a watery mix of Ultramarine and Crimson. Paint the roof of the long shed on the left with your size No. 2 nylon brush and White plus touches of Coeruleum Blue and Cadmium Yellow. Paint the brick buildings with Crimson, Cadmium Yellow and a little White. Use Coeruleum Blue, Cadmium Yellow and plenty of White for the warship to the right of the ferry. Put in the *Victory*'s masts with your Series 56, size No. 1 sable and ox brush, using thin, watery paint. Add small amounts of detail to the buildings with light and dark colours.

Third stage Now we are ready to start on the water. Use your size No. 6 nylon brush and the sky colours. Work down the canvas from the distant buildings. Use plenty of White at first and add more colour as you proceed. Work in horizontal brush strokes. Paint the area of oily water where the ferry has turned away from the jetty with downwards strokes, using the watercolour-type treatment illustrated in **figs. 18** and **19**, page 24. Finally, put in some reflected sunlight to the right of the ferry with White and Cadmium Yellow.

Fourth stage This is the meaty part of the painting – the ferry. Start by painting the mast with your size No. 6 sable brush and a mix of Ultramarine, Crimson and a little Cadmium Yellow. Paint the funnel with your size No. 2 nylon brush and Coeruleum Blue, Cadmium Yellow and White. Paint the cabin under the funnel, using White and a touch of Cadmium Yellow for the sunny side. Add a little Ultramarine and Crimson and use less White for the shadow side. When this has dried put in the door on the side of the cabin, using the mast colours. Also use these colours for the underside of the canopy. Use Cadmium Red and Cadmium Yellow to paint the two boxes on the side of the funnel. Put in the figures on the boat with your size No. 6 sable brush. Paint the heads first, using Cadmium Red, Cadmium Yellow and White. Work down from the heads, using various colours to suit the mood of your painting. Use positive downwards strokes. If the figure is facing away from you, cover the pink face you have painted, but in some cases leave a little showing at the neck. To paint a figure in profile, put a dark colour on top of the face for hair or a cap and continue your brush strokes down to form the clothed body. These figures are only suggested but, painted with freedom and confidence, they are just what is needed. Paint the dark areas to the left

First stage

Second stage

Third stage

Fourth stage

Finished stage
41 × 30cm (16 × 12in)

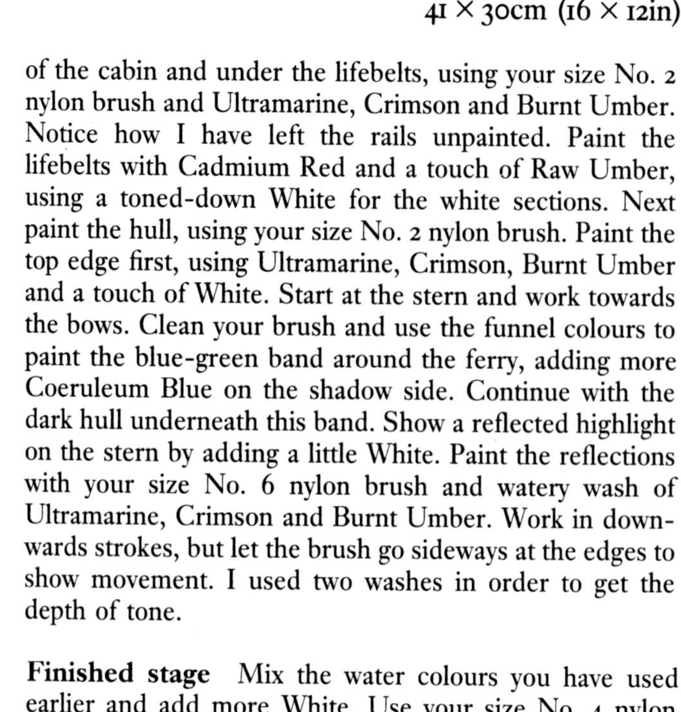

of the cabin and under the lifebelts, using your size No. 2 nylon brush and Ultramarine, Crimson and Burnt Umber. Notice how I have left the rails unpainted. Paint the lifebelts with Cadmium Red and a touch of Raw Umber, using a toned-down White for the white sections. Next paint the hull, using your size No. 2 nylon brush. Paint the top edge first, using Ultramarine, Crimson, Burnt Umber and a touch of White. Start at the stern and work towards the bows. Clean your brush and use the funnel colours to paint the blue-green band around the ferry, adding more Coeruleum Blue on the shadow side. Continue with the dark hull underneath this band. Show a reflected highlight on the stern by adding a little White. Paint the reflections with your size No. 6 nylon brush and watery wash of Ultramarine, Crimson and Burnt Umber. Work in downwards strokes, but let the brush go sideways at the edges to show movement. I used two washes in order to get the depth of tone.

Finished stage Mix the water colours you have used earlier and add more White. Use your size No. 4 nylon brush to work the water over and into the reflection, with short, horizontal strokes. Work the lighter water colours from left to right and right to left over the reflection. Imagine the water, feeling it moving and swirling as you paint. Let the brush jump and move around, as though it were in water. Put highlights on the people in the ferry. Paint the canopy supports, rails and rigging with your Series 56, size No. 1 sable and ox brush. Use a mix of Ultramarine, Crimson and a touch of Cadmium Yellow, adding plenty of White for the lighter-coloured areas. Show the edge of the canopy with White and a little Raw Umber. Put some darks and lights on the harbour buildings and paint the yachts to the left of the ferry. Add more highlights to the water to the right of the boats, and to the edge of the dark clouds above the funnel. Put in a whiff of smoke coming out of the funnel. Look at your picture later with a fresh eye, adding any highlights and darks you then feel are necessary.

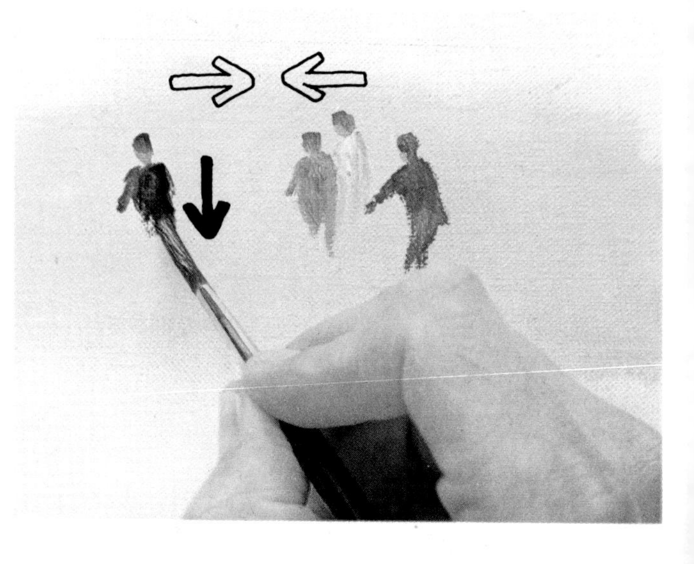

First stage

Second stage

Third stage

EXERCISE SEVEN
FISHING VILLAGE
IN PEN AND PASTEL

I originally painted this exercise in watercolour at Lympstone, a little village on the Exe estuary in Devon. The poles in the foreground and next to the houses are for hanging the fishing nets out to dry, and there is often washing drying on them, too! The tide goes down and you can walk out to them without wearing waders. It was a good watercolour subject, because of the contrast of the poles against the light water, but I decided to try pen with pastel painted over it, using my watercolour painting as my working information sketch. I used a fountain pen with black Indian ink and worked on GREENS RWS 140lb HOT PRESSED watercolour paper.

First stage Draw the picture first in HB pencil. This will give you confidence when you work over it with your pen. Don't put detail in with the pencil. Draw over the buildings on the left with your pen, then add the poles, boats and distant hills. Work on the foreground boats and hand-cart. Don't try to copy your pencil lines slavishly with the pen, use them only as a guide. Do not try to create a single, perfect pen line. Let the pen work freely, even if you draw two or three lines instead of one. This will give character to the drawing.

Second stage Use your size No. 6 sable brush and black ink diluted with water (put some ink in a mixing palette or on a saucer – don't put water into your full ink bottle). Start with the background, using very watery ink, and then paint the rocks in the middle-distance. Continue to the right of them in one brush stroke across the water, to give tone to this area. Work on the trees, houses and poles, creating different tone values by adding water to your ink. Use undiluted ink for most of the foreground and the area under the two left-hand rowing boats. Finish with some free, horizontal brush strokes on the beach. Let the brush jump up and down, leaving white paper to suggest stones.

Third stage Work from left to right on the distant hills, using Sap Green Tint 3 and Green Grey Tint 6. Add Burnt Umber Tint 4 and smudge these colours together in places. Next paint the buildings: use Yellow Ochre Tint 2 for the light yellow areas; Burnt Umber Tint 4 for the brown areas, and Cadmium Red Tint 4 for the roofs and the pink house – for this put only a little on and rub it in with your finger. Paint the sea wall underneath the houses

Finished stage 36 × 48cm (14 × 19in)

with Green Grey Tint 6. Merge it into some houses above with your finger. For the side wall of the nearest house, use Burnt Umber Tint 4, and paint over it with Green Grey Tint 6. Apply the pastel lightly where you want some of the ink wash to show through. Rub it with your finger if you want a smooth effect. You create another tone with the pastel by allowing the background to show through. Use Cobalt Blue Tint 2 for the nearest windows. Next put in the reflections. Paint the middle-distance rocks with Burnt Umber Tint 4 and Green Grey Tint 6. Rub these colours in with your finger.

Finished stage Paint the poles with Burnt Umber Tint 4, Sap Green Tint 3 and Green Grey Tint 6. Put in the left-hand boat with Burnt Umber Tint 4. Use Cobalt Blue Tint 2 for the blue boat and Sap Green Tint 3 for the bottom. Paint the white boat with Yellow Ochre Tint 2. Use all your pastels, except Cadmium Red Tint 4 and Cobalt Blue Tint 2, for the beach. Paint it with long, horizontal strokes, rubbing it and merging colours with your fingers. Use these colours for the hand-cart. If you overdo the pastel or want to take some off your picture, remove it with a putty rubber or bristle brush. Use your pen to add crispness by working over any area you want, picking out detail. Finally, with your pen, put in the ropes fastened round the net poles.

DO'S AND DON'TS

DO NOT USE ACRYLIC COLOUR OVER OIL COLOUR

DO NOT PUT IN TOO MUCH DETAIL WHILE YOU ARE LEARNING

DO NOT WORRY TOO MUCH ABOUT TECHNICAL DETAIL

REMEMBER THAT WATER MUST APPEAR HORIZONTAL

REMEMBER THAT THE SKY CONVEYS THE MOOD OF THE PAINTING

BUY THE BEST MATERIALS YOU CAN AFFORD

VARY THE AMOUNTS OF COLOUR USED IN A MIXTURE

DO NOT BE AFRAID TO USE PHOTOGRAPHS – AS AN AID

REMEMBER THAT OBSERVATION IS THE KEY TO GOOD PAINTING

ENJOY YOUR PAINTING, REMEMBER THAT IT'S FUN

AND TAKE IT EASY – PRACTISE, PRACTISE, PRACTISE AND DON'T RUN BEFORE YOU CAN WALK!!

GLOSSARY

Amidships: in the middle of a boat
Beam: width of the boat at its widest part
Boom: horizontal spar that holds the bottom of the mainsail
Bow: front of a boat
Hull: body of a boat
Jib: triangular sail stretching forward from the mast
Lee-board: frame of planks, fixed to the side of a flat-bottomed boat, lowered to control the boat's leeward drift
Leeward: the side or direction away from the wind
Mainsail: large sail set on the main mast
Mast: vertical pole for supporting the sails
Port: left side of a boat when facing forward
Rigging: all the ropes and lines of a boat
Rudder: underwater steering gear at the stern
Sheet: line used to adjust a sail
Starboard: right side of a boat when facing forward
Stays: mast supports
Stern: back of a boat